# Women and Computers

## Frances Grundy
### with John Grundy

Cartoons by Angela Martin

**intellect**™

First Published in 1996 by
**Intellect Books**
EFAE, Earl Richards Road North, Exeter EX2 6AS

Consulting editor:   Masoud Yazdani
Copy editor:         Wendy Momen
Cover cartoon:       Angela Martin
Proofreader:         Rachel Andrews

**A catalogue record for this book is available from the British Library**

ISBN 1-871516-36-6

Printed and bound in Great Britain by Cromwell Press, Wiltshire

# Contents

# Acknowledgements

It has now fully dawned on me that it is impossible to write a book like this on one's own. Colleagues, students, friends, family all provide ideas, some by dint of hard work and some rather more inadvertently!

I owe a particular debt of gratitude to Barbara Segal and Dave Woodall for their insightful criticisms of an early draft. Alison Adam and Hyacinth Nwana too were both very helpfully critical. An anonymous referee made some useful suggestions which have made Chapter 6 easier reading. Louise Moses made helpful comments which led to some points being more intelligible for readers from outside the UK. Wendy Richards has been extremely supportive and a valuable advisor throughout this venture. And others have provided comments and ideas which helped improve and sharpen it, including Brenda Banks, Dean Brown, Sarah Grundy and Karen Gunter.

My thanks are due to all those secretaries and some of the other staff in Computer Science departments who responded, some with great care, to my request for information about university departments.

Athula Herath's skill, knowledge of typesetting software and his generosity with his time helped me enormously in the preparation of this text for printing.

My initial ideas for the three levels of criticism and solution, which form the basis for Part IV of this book, were first presented at a Women into Computing Conference in 1992. This paper was subsequently published in the international journal GATES (Greater Access to Technology, Engineering and Science) in 1994. My observations about the workplace and some of my ideas flowing from that, which appear in Chapters 4 and 5, were first presented at the Women, Work and Computerization Conference held in Manchester, England in 1994.

Finally, Angela Martin's cartoons greatly cheered the final stages of the writing of this book, as I have no doubt they will the reading of it.

To all those women who have been, and will be, cheated
of the chance of a decent career simply for being women

*The social subordination of women . . . stands out an isolated
fact in modern social institutions . . . a single relic of an old
world of thought and practice exploded in everything else,
but retained in one thing of most universal interest; as if a
gigantic dolmen, or a vast temple of Jupiter Olympius, occupied the site of St Paul's and received daily worship . . .*

John Stuart Mill 1869

# Part I

# Laying the Foundations

# 1

# What I Mean by 'Feminism'

*It is agreeable to [men] that men should live for their own sake, women for the sake of men . . .* Harriet Taylor Mill 1851 (Mill 1970a, p107)

## 1.1 'Feminism' Made Simple

It came as a surprise to me to find that there was sufficient material on women and computing to fill even a short book like this one. Whenever I have tried to raise the subject, those around me denied there was a problem, became irritated by my persistence or simply looked the other way, embarrassed by my determination to break a taboo. The question of women's role in computing was a non-question that somehow didn't exist or, if it did, was not worthy of discussion. For all that time I accepted the tacit argument that the very low numbers of women in the profession and in the classes I taught was itself evidence that there was nothing to discuss.

It is indeed amazing what women have accepted. For instance, one would have thought that if any activity was essentially a woman's province, bearing children would be it – and yet for over two centuries men have not only dominated but virtually monopolised the treatment of women in the fields of obstetrics and gynaecology. And this Alice in Wonderland situation has gone largely unchallenged by women; yet if anyone should dominate this area it should surely be them. But the subject of this book is computing and information technology and there is no obvious reason why either gender should dominate this territory; it belongs equally to both.

However, I developed an increasing sense of alienation towards a subject I had entered with enthusiasm in the 1960s. I began to realise that maybe it wasn't so much my fault that I felt out of place, that it was nothing I had done or failed to do. Rather it was never intended that I should be 'in place'; powerful patriarchal influences were determined to ensure that I, and other women like me, were merely tolerated guests. This situation seems to me to be fundamentally wrong.

There is a multi-layered ideology underlying my view of this situation. The first layer is based on the belief that there is no difference between the intelligence, abilities and aptitude of women and those of men, that all jobs should be open to everyone regardless of their gender, and people should be chosen purely on merit. This equality of opportunity and of ability and the equal right of women to take up any job for which they are fitted might be called *minimal feminism*. This first layer of feminism does not include the idea that women are superior and more able than men, either by nature or by upbringing. Nor, in order to fit this definition, does one have to demand extreme measures to bring about the end of this inequality. But to be a feminist under this minimal definition one does have to believe that women are inherently equal to men and that equality of opportunity should be the norm.

Many women shrink in horror from the idea of being labelled 'feminist'. For example, I hear them say, 'We are not feminist, we are feminine'. The word 'feminist' of course means so many different things to different people. It needs to be pinned down, say to this minimal definition, before you can know the meaning of statements like 'I am not feminist' or 'I am a feminist'. Pinning down the definition of 'feminist' to, for instance, this minimal definition does make it clear that someone who denies she is a feminist in this sense must be denying one of two things. Either she is denying that women are equal to men in ability and aptitudes, or she is denying that people should have equality of opportunity and is suggesting that people should be given jobs on the basis of their gender rather than on merit.

Minimal feminism stresses that women are equal in ability and that jobs should be given on merit. This should result in a situation where jobs and people are matched according to their talents and according to their aptitudes and interests. This would mean that people were not only highly productive but also more fulfilled as individuals.

What has happened over a long period of time amounts to a pincer movement. On the one hand jobs become gendered: 'these jobs are suitable for women'; on the other the genders are channelled into jobs: 'women are suitable for these jobs'. This is not meant to imply that all types of jobs are perfectly gendered but that jobs are regarded to varying degrees as being more appropriate for one gender than the other. In other words, there are different degrees of *job-gendering* and of course the degree to which a job is gendered varies over time. For example, nurses are no longer exclusively female nor are bus drivers any longer exclusively male. But you would still be hard-pressed to find examples of male nursery nurses. Until very recently you most certainly would not have found a female Anglican priest in this country. And many male Anglican priests are so attached to this old exclusive gendering that, now it is abolished, they are prepared to leave the Church of England and become priests of other denominations. In the Roman Catholic church the job of priest is still perfectly gendered.

The other half of the dual action is *gender-channelling*. Girls are brought up to regard themselves as more suited to child-rearing, nursing, hairdressing and typing. It is still usually regarded as 'tom-boyish' and inappropriate by their teachers and parents, and not least by the girls themselves, for a girl to want to be an engineer in oily overalls.

Computing is not immune from job-gendering nor are women immune from gender-channelling with respect to computing. There are efforts on the part of men – it is irrelevant whether these efforts are conscious and deliberate or not – to project an image of computing which is masculine. It is the effects of this that I and women like me experience when we feel that we are merely tolerated guests in male territory.

The combined action of job-gendering and gender-channelling greatly hampers, and indeed in some cases entirely prevents, the process of an individual taking up the work to which he or she is most suited. This, to varying degrees, prevents self-fulfilment of individuals – individuals of both genders – and of course leads to a massive waste of talent. Feminism, as I conceive it, is an ideology which in putting this right will benefit both genders, not just women, though of course it does mean the end of exclusive rights for men to certain types and levels of job.

The second layer of this ideology, which I would like to call *optimal feminism*, embraces all that minimal feminism asserts but goes further. Minimal feminism only claims for women that they are equal to men. Optimal feminism, on the other hand, claims that most women are by their upbringing and training, but not inherently by their nature, able to bring certain attitudes and motivations to work which are more valuable than the attitudes and motivations that men bring. The general ethos of the working environment created by men is one where the primary motive is self-aggrandisement through control of others, either directly or indirectly through things like money and equipment. In fact this motive is more important than getting the work done. Other aspects of this ethos are competitiveness of a counter-productive sort, unnecessary hierarchies or people having managers when they can manage their own work more efficiently by themselves. And there is a tendency to centre power in people who are not accountable for their actions and who do not share decision making with others.

Women tend to avoid this counter-productive competitiveness. An example of another component of this cluster of attitudes is to be found in that enduringly macho world, the police force. Women report how they see their male colleagues rush into delicate situations with aggression, situations into which the women tend to go in a negotiating mode (Critical Eye 1994). The policemen disempower in order to gain submissive control; the policewomen offer empowerment through negotiation in order to achieve consensual control.

There is a tendency for women to be more caring and nurturing than men, hence their preponderance in counselling roles, in nursing, catering and other types of domestic work. It is this nurturing aspect of women that gives rise to feminist politics which is the subject of a chapter in the final part of this book.

Of course not all women have these attitudes, nor do all men have the attitudes I have ascribed to them. In other words, I am not saying that all women are angels and all men are devils. There are many women who enjoy the cut-and-thrust of what I have called counter-productive competitiveness; there are many women who do not have a nurturing disposition. So too there are many men who latently have the traits I have labelled as feminine and would be much happier if they practised them. But they are caught up in this masculine world where to exhibit such traits can only work to their disadvantage. A useful parallel here is the notion of 'western ideas'.

We often talk of a western idea, but no one would ever infer that all westerners have such an idea or that such ideas are not found elsewhere. So clearly some men think in the way I have labelled as feminine and some women think in the way I have called masculine.

It is important at this point to clear up one possible misunderstanding of some of the things I shall be saying and at the same time to develop further my definition of optimal feminism and its implications. At times I talk about activities being masculine or feminine. For instance, I talk of science and engineering as we know them being inherently masculine; on the other hand I talk in terms of housework being feminine. And it might look as if I am endorsing the *status quo* and saying that men ought to go into science and engineering and women stay at home to do the housework. (Or, as one sympathetic commentator observed 'Come back Janet and John, all is forgiven!') But of course when I describe certain jobs as masculine and others as feminine, I do this within the context of the present job-gendering and gender-channelling. By various means some jobs come to be thought of as belonging to one gender rather than the other. And at the same time each gender seems to be more suited to one set of jobs rather than others. But of course on a minimal feminist view no job is either masculine or feminine and the genders are not suited to a particular range of jobs.

Indeed what minimal feminism demands is the abolition of all job-gendering and gender-channelling. This would remove the bias these factors introduce and make it much easier for individuals to choose each for her- or himself what is most suitable for them as individuals.

Optimal feminism complicates this picture considerably. It recognises that women, because of their upbringing and training, bring to their work a set of attitudes preferable to those brought by men. Consequently, optimal feminism is committed to the idea that, in the long run at any rate, both boys and girls should be brought up in the way girls are at present. This is not to say that men and women should adopt the whole gamut of the way that girls are now brought up to think and feel. Men should be brought up to adopt the feminine characteristics I have just outlined but not, for example, the dependency that girls have traditionally been taught to feel.

In a sense, this means the end of gender-channelling just as much as minimal feminism means the same, but in a different way. Gender-channelling gets its meaning from the contrast in the way one gender is channelled as compared with the way the other gender is channelled. (Compare this with the way in which in order to establish a sense of one's own identity one needs to interact with others.) In other words, if both genders are 'channelled' in the same way, there is in effect no gender-channelling.

This helps with an apparent difficulty. I appear on the one hand to be saying job-gendering and gender-channelling are bad things; on the other hand I appear to be advocating the kind of job-gendering and gender-channelling that produce women's present attitude to their work. This at first sight is contradictory. But the main reason why I criticise job-gendering and gender-channelling is that they restrict people's freedom, mainly the freedom of women. It is as if women were being told 'You can go in for this restricted range of jobs, while men may choose from all the rest'. If people were brought up in the way I am advocating, they would all take to their work the present attitude of most women but both genders would be able to choose from the full range of jobs. In this way optimal feminism aims to get the best of both worlds.

Anticipating a further possible misunderstanding might throw more light on the implications of optimal feminism. I have talked as though one of the valuable results of a feminist programme would be the much greater opportunity for individuals to be themselves, including being quite free to choose those jobs that suit them best, thus allowing individualism to flourish. Two issues arise here. One is that this individualism might be seen to be of the 'each for himself' kind – an aggressive and greedy ethos. Secondly, it might seem contradictory to talk of giving individuals their freedom to act without external pressures and, at the same time, to talk of social engineering to bring them up to have the same set of attitudes and motivations as girls are brought up to have at present.

But the implementation of the optimal feminism I have in mind meets both these objections. To deal with the second first: no one supposes that bringing up children to have moral scruples and to have respect for the law and for other people makes anything but a relatively small and very acceptable inroad on their individuality. For those brought up to share concern and care for others, there is huge scope for the flowering of individual differences. This also answers the first of the two objections. Talk of flourishing individualism does not mean a licence for people to compete in a destructive way. My view of optimal feminism is fundamentally one in which individuals would be brought up to be more caring and nurturing than men are at present.

But some would ask, why stop at optimal feminism, why not take what looks like the next logical step to what I shall call *drastic feminism*? The difference between drastic and optimal feminism is that drastic feminists argue that women are inherently superior, that the tables should be turned and that they should dominate in much the same way that men dominate at present.[1]

It is not my belief that women are inherently superior; there is no evidence to suggest this. Therefore I have no reason to take the further step towards drastic feminism. Evidently there is a spectrum of feminist views and being feminist in any sense of the word does not mean that one has to hold the views of either extreme of the spectrum.

It goes without saying that there are many aspects of these definitions and their implications which require such lengthy investigation that there would be no space in this present book to discuss women and computing. There is moreover some merit in leaving the definition at a clear and simple, though hopefully not simplistic, level.

---

[1] There are of course other, more complex classifications of different viewpoints within feminism which are useful for other purposes. Rosemarie Tong (1989), for example, distinguishes liberal, Marxist, radical, psycho-analytic, socialist, existentialist and postmodern feminism.

## 1.2   This Book

This book is about women's attitudes towards computers and the activity of computing, whether it be as a clerk inputting data, a young girl seeing her brother playing computer games and not able or wanting to join in, a secretary being asked to type and retype something her boss could do just as easily himself, or a girl seeing a computer for the first time and wondering what it implications it has for her. It is about a young woman starting a computing course in a university, a schoolgirl embarking on a secondary level computing course. It is also about the housewife who wonders why it is that when all around her things are becoming more and more automated, and while the changes in domestic technology appear at first sight to be quite exciting, in practice for her nothing has changed.

Much of the material I have used for this book is drawn from my experiences in several computing jobs. For the most part these have been in a university setting, first as a computing advisor and latterly as a lecturer. I recently spent twelve months working on secondment in the computing department of a District Health Authority writing some database systems. This experience gave me a fresh opportunity to observe men and women in the computing workplace. Working for a short period in an unfamiliar organisation gave me a spectator's view of what was happening in my immediate surroundings. It did not, however, give me insight into the long term prospects for women in this type of environment. My observations on this aspect of working life have to be drawn mainly from my university experiences.

Chapter 2 describes how girls' upbringing in general sets the scene for their future disadvantaged role in the use of computers and, in particular, the part that computer games play in these early stages. These early influences encourage a different approach to computing on the part of girls than that taken by boys. There are all sorts of factors influencing attitudes to computers, for instance levels of anxiety, experience and achievement, gender and age. I discuss some of these and examine a little of what has been written on them.

Unlike men's work, 'women's work', by which I mean housework, household management, childcare and the like, is never aided by the use of computers to the extent that enough time is saved to release the houseworker to do alternative work. 'Computers in the home' normally implies games, entertainment and perhaps the odd micro-computer in a central heating system, burglar alarm or washing machine. Chapter 3 gives a brief overview of the development of domestic technology and its real benefit to housewives and asks, and offers some tentative answers to, the question: 'Why are there so few computers in the home?'

Part III describes the situation within computing as it exists now. Readers, both women and men, might compare their own experiences with what I have described. No doubt many will recognise situations similar to those in which they work. Many will have examples and anecdotes of their own and probably 'angles' I have not included.

In Chapter 4 I give an account of some things that I observed in the District Health Authority – some of the behavioural patterns that contribute to the marginalisation of women in the computing workplace, the downgrading of their work and the corresponding upgrading of men's work. Following on from this, Chapter 5 examines the differences in types of work – the 'pure' and the 'messy' – and the role that computer hardware plays in the stratification of computer-related work. I have introduced the phrase *sexist skill evaluation* to describe the phenomenon of how women's jobs are undervalued simply because women do them and, of course, the contrasting evaluation of men's jobs.

Chapters 6 and 7 are about education. Chapter 6 sketches the background against which girls and women progressively opt out of computing courses so that the number of women studying computer science at undergraduate level is very small. It is also about teaching at all levels but particularly at that of which I have most experience – higher education. It is about the academic teaching profession from two angles: first, in Chapter 6 I look at how the profession is structured and the forces at work in the structuring process; secondly, in Chapter 7 I discuss how we teach our students and the ways in which some of our techniques, in particular our use of language, affect women students.

Given the way everything is apparently 'stitched up' from 'A' level [2] to university and beyond, what hope is there for change? The presence of strong taboos against talking about, let alone publishing anything on, the topic of women and computing acts as an effective deterrent to change. Chapter 8 looks in more detail at how these deterrents stifle the birth of new ideas, particularly in the field of publishing. Feminist literature has some effect, but the ideas propagated in this literary stream seem to be taking an inordinately long time to enter everyday use in the world of computing.

When once asked for my reasons for suggesting something to my head of department in the 1970s I responded that my reasons were intuitive. 'We can't possibly rely on intuition!' was the riposte. Intuition does have a place and men use it too, although they may well use it in different ways. Chapter 9 is a rebuttal of the classic argument that men only use intelligence and women intuition and that the former is superior to the latter.

Part IV suggests three levels at which the present situation might change for the better. These are three levels of criticism and solution. The first, described in Chapter 10, is that of 'adding-more-women'. Without more women, nothing can change. But this is not enough; there have to be other changes as well. Chapter 11 is concerned with the second level of criticism, which is called the 'liberal' level. This is about qualitative changes: to the environment in which we practise and teach computing and in the application of computing for morally worthy ends. All this is in the light of the feminist politics generated by what I have called 'optimal feminism'. Finally, the 'radical' level is introduced in Chapter 12. This is where we start looking for a really new science and encouraging a transformation not only of the way we do it, but also what it is that we do.

---

[2]Schoolchildren in England, Wales and Northern Ireland normally take a General Certificate of Secondary Education, or GCSE, at 16 years of age after two years of study. 'A', or Advanced level, is taken after two further years of study. Normally, three 'A' levels are needed to qualify for university entrance.

# Part II

# Chips with Everything . . .

# 2

# ... But not for Girls

*As long as boys and girls run about in the dirt, and trundle hoops together, they are both precisely alike. If you catch up one-half of these creatures and train them to a particular set of actions and opinions, and the other half to a perfectly opposite set, of course their understandings will differ ... There is surely no occasion to go into any deeper or more abstruse reasoning, in order to explain so very simple a phenomenon.* Sydney Smith 1840, quoted by Harriet Taylor Mill (Smith 1840, p200)

## 2.1   Janet and John's First Steps

Play is as important in the computing culture as it is in any other and, as in so many other contexts, games and play are a good deal more serious and influential than they seem. We talk, for instance, of kittens playing games, when in fact much of that is preparation for the deadly serious activities of hunting and defence later on. In just the same way children's play and the games it involves are, and are meant to be, very much a preparation for adult life.

Of course not all things children play with are chosen by their parents or other adults; children will make for mud and saucepan lids quite independently. But a great number of playthings are chosen by adults. And it is an obvious and well known fact that there are systematically different themes for the games adults choose for boys on the one hand and those they choose for girls on the other. Perhaps boys and girls do have very similar fluffy toys and rattles to begin with, and as they grow there will, of course, be some gender neutral playthings such as building blocks, paints, etc. But they are not very many months old by the time the boys are given toy cars, trains and so on and the girls are given dolls. Indeed this process starts well before birth for many of them. How many fathers, for instance, wish for a son in order to be able to give him train sets and take him fishing? There is a whole range of toys and games given to one gender rather than the other. The range for each tends to have a distinct and differentiating theme.

The boys have train sets, meccano, lego, working models of steam engines, radio controlled model cars and so on. Toys and games such as these obviously help boys to become familiar with and confident in constructing things, operating them and finding out how they work. Another obvious major theme in what boys are given is that of violence and aggression. They are given guns, swords, Action Men, commando type outfits – all geared to violence, competition and winning.

Girls, on the other hand, are given dolls (some complete with babies' bottles for feeding and tears to wipe), dolls' houses, prams, toy cookers, nurses' outfits – all geared to nurturing and looking after the needs of others. They are, moreover, games where competition and winning just don't enter the scene.

In these ways a gap is created between that with which each gender is familiar and confident. This gap is widened by boys and girls seeing their fathers with their heads deep inside the car bonnet and, when the washing machine needs repair, seeing a man come to fix it – never a woman. As far as sophistication in engineering goes, all they see their mothers doing is pressing buttons. This theme, which will be elaborated in the next chapter, is important. There is evidence that people with more seriously negative attitudes towards computers were more likely to have been introduced to their mechanical experience by their mothers, who 'they see retrospectively as having been uncomfortable with machinery' (Weil, Rosen and Wugalter 1990, p373).

It is important to note that these influences not only strengthen the idea that certain activities are appropriate for boys and men and certain others for girls and women but also that, by and large, those permitted for one gender are outside the range of activities permitted for the other.


## 2.2   The Game's the Thing

Well before children reach their teens, the scene is set for computer games to help widen the gap between the genders. There are three main ways this happens – the differing levels of attraction that the *content* of computer games have for boys and girls, the different levels of *confidence* with which boys and girls approach them and the *social context* in which they are played.


### Content and Sex Appeal

Practically all computer games pick up and continue the theme of destruction and violence which we saw in many of the games for younger boys. The majority are about winning and in particular they are war games of the 'beat-em-up-shoot-em-up' variety. So the content of most computer games is designed to appeal exclusively to boys. I say exclusively because these destructive games run quite counter to the nurturing theme of girls' games and play activities. And it needs to be kept in mind that a sign against a certain range of activities reading 'This is for you, boys!' is tantamount to saying 'Girls keep out!'.

It is not surprising that the adults who give toys with the different themes I have just mentioned to their sons and daughters should perceive computer games as, on the whole, suitable for boys but not for girls. Boys thus have parental blessing for playing them.

The reaction against destruction of things and people on the part of girls is likely to be accentuated by the increasing realism which better and better graphics make possible. In early games like *Space Invaders* what the player destroyed was an almost diagrammatic little icon and it wasn't even clear if what one saw destroyed was the living thing itself or a sort of vehicle containing the living thing. More and more often these days the blood and guts (and occasional eyeball) splattered across the screen make clear that it is a living thing that one has just destroyed. Most girls and women will say, 'Not for me, thank you'.

It seems likely that considerable experience and confidence in playing computer games confer substantial advantage in later study and work with computers. At present all this advantage seems to go to the boys because the content of most games deters girls. Are there any games, apart from *Barbie Goes Shopping*, *Solitaire*, *Tetris* and *Sim City* and its derivatives, that are written for girls rather than boys? (I have just seen in a computer magazine a cartoon picturing, in one half, a stand packed with games of the usual type for boys and, in the other half, a stand empty apart from a single game for girls called *Barbie in Fluffyland*(PC Format 1995).)

## 'He Who Dares Wins'

We have just seen how the content of games widens the gap between boys and girls and now turn to the way in which confidence, or lack of it, widens this gap even further.

One of the effects of marking out an area of activity as appropriate for boys and encouraging them to be active in it, is that they soon build up a high level of confidence in that area. Marcia Linn (1985) reports how American junior high school students (usually aged 12 to 14) were given two games, called *Wumpus* and *Rocky's Boots*, to play. In *Wumpus* the player searches through rooms looking for the *Wumpus* in order to shoot it with an arrow. In the search for the *Wumpus* the player has continually to avoid the threat of being killed. In *Rocky's Boots* the student has to design a machine constructed from logic gates. The machine then tries to identify objects and signifies recognition by kicking them.

Male and female students consistently differed in four respects in their approaches to playing these games. The first of these was that, in both games, boys were more likely to go beyond the information given and to test the rules to their limits in order to understand them. Girls, on the other hand, did as they were instructed which meant in some cases proceeding with caution and avoiding risks which might have given them more information.

Secondly, boys were more realistic in predicting the outcome of their work, particularly successful outcomes. They were also optimistic about outcomes that turned out to be unsuccessful. Girls, on the other hand, were more pessimistic about outcomes, successful or otherwise.

Thirdly, boys attributed their success to the use of a good strategy, that is to their ability; girls, on the other hand, attributed most of their success to luck, that is they did not attribute their success to their own ability. Girls attributed their failure to personal lack of competence, whereas boys looked for more specific reasons. This finding is consistent with that of Valerie Clarke and Susan Chambers in a different context. In a group of students doing a compulsory computing course at the tertiary level they found that 'Men rated their own ability more highly as a possible reason for their success, while women rated their own lack of ability more highly as a possible source of failure' (Clarke and Chambers 1989, p421).

Finally, the girls sought help from the experimenters more often than the boys did. Some discussions I have had with graduate students who assist in undergraduate practical laboratories for computing courses servicing other subjects (as opposed to mainstream computer science) confirm this final phenomenon, although not in the context of playing games. The women, when stuck, tend to put up their hands and ask for help, rather than try things out, which is what the men tend to do.

Marcia Linn's study strongly suggests that, even by the time they reach 12 to 14, girls have much less confidence than the boys in handling entertainments like *Wumpus* and *Rocky's Boots* and, consequently, girls find them off-putting. This dissuades them from entering into the computer learning process that computer games offer, a process which seems, at present, to be one major route towards a further involvement in computing. So this early confidence on the part of the boys is something they build on, enhancing their progress in computing, while girls' lack of confidence has the opposite effect.

> Unto everyone that hath shall be given and he shall have abundance: but from him that hath not shall be taken away even that which he hath.[1]


## Girls and Boys Come Out to Play . . .

Now we turn to the third way in which games tend to widen the gap between boys and girls – the social context in which they are played.

I said at the beginning of this chapter that children's games are a very important preparation for the serious activity of adult life. To explain how this works in the case of boys let us look at a study by Janet Lever (1976) of 181 5th-grade children (10 and 11 year olds) in which she found several important differences in the ways the two sexes played. Boys played out of doors more frequently than girls, and played more often in large groups of mixed ages. Their games were more often competitive and they lasted longer than girls' games. This longer lastingness appeared to be for two reasons. One was that boys' games required a high level of skill and were thus less likely to become tedious. The other reason suggested was that disputes were arising all the time in the course of a game and boys were able to resolve these disputes very effectively. Indeed the boys seemed to enjoy the legal debates as much as they did the games themselves. Even those who didn't play the games very well joined in as equals in these disputes.

---

[1] Matt 25:29, hence this has been called by some wit 'the Matthew effect'.

Through this sort of game-playing, boys develop considerable skill and interest in the elaboration of rules for adjudicating conflicts. Rules are accepted by all sides if only because they are often biased to the strongest boy or team. By using such rules, disruptions of the games can be minimised by giving the boys a way to deal with disputes effectively. Carol Gilligan (1993, p10) who cites Lever's work, points out that Lever's discussion of the results is shaped by the assumption that the male model is the better one, since it fits the requirements for modern corporate success. This, as Gilligan goes on to say, contrasts with the low market value of the sensitivity and care for the feelings of others that girls develop through their play and elsewhere. Indeed their care and sensitivity may be a disadvantage to their professional success.

Girls' games, like skipping in a group, hop-scotch and cat's cradle, are 'turn-taking' and thus much less competitive. Janet Lever found that most of the girls in her study broke off a game if a serious dispute arose, on the grounds that avoiding risk to relationships was more important than continuing the game. So the opportunities for learning how to settle disputes and minimise disruption to games did not arise. In fact Luria (1981), as quoted by Jean Baker Miller (1991), found that girls often remain on the periphery of the playground in smaller, more intimate groups, often just two best friends. When she asked girls what they were doing, they often said 'nothing', they were 'just talking'. What they dismissed as 'just talking' turned out to be discussions of issues in their families and how to solve them, discussions which meant that they were 'very involved in an emotional interaction with one another' (Baker Miller 1991, p19).

To get back to computer games, it is clear that they are, for a start, not the type of game that would enable boys to become skilled at resolving disputes. It is true there is some element of competition among players in that sometimes games are played by more than one player at once; or, when played by individuals sequentially, players often compare scores or levels reached. Nevertheless they are largely played by individuals and, though the element of competition is strong – usually a matter of either kill or be killed – the competition is more between the player and his machine rather than among players. So, there is little of the interaction with others that would enable players to develop dispute-solving skills. Indeed there is little opportunity for the development of any social skills through interaction. And the widespread worry is that boys are substituting computer games for the kinds of activities that previously enabled them to develop social skills and relationships (EIU 1993). The individuality and separateness of the boys in the football games was at least tempered by membership of teams and the need to resolve disputes. In computer games that team membership and need to resolve disputes have largely disappeared.

So there are two different but very closely related reasons why girls should say 'No thank you' to computer games. One involves individuality and separateness in the games themselves and the other, which is intertwined with the first, involves that same individuality and separateness but this time in the social context in which the games are played. I have already commented a number of times on the separateness and lack of caring so essential to the content of the kill or be killed games. The competition between player and machine takes the most war-like and uncaring of forms. If the limited amount of competition among players holds little attraction for girls who find their identity in caring relationships, they must find the death and destruction in the games themselves deeply alien. In fact this world of death and destruction and the largely solitary way it is practised is the very opposite of the kind of world in which girls and women not only find their identity in caring interaction with others, but also fulfilment and enjoyment (Baker Miller 1991). Girls and women find their identity and fulfilment 'through connection' rather than 'through separation', through caring empathic relationships rather than through the individuation and independence that leads to the separation associated with masculinity (Gilligan 1993).

This introduces the second manifestation of separateness and individuality, but this time manifested in the social context. A US study paints a picture that seems to sum up a lot of this. The boys are to be found in the video arcades playing electronic games individually. Occasionally they bring their girl friends who are there to admire and applaud their boy friends' performance rather than play the games themselves. The majority of the girls are in adjacent restaurants and snack bars (Kiesler, Sproull and Eccles 1985), just as we noted earlier they were on the periphery of the playground.

There seem to me to be two processes at work here. The boys are strengthening bonds amongst themselves through shared knowledge about the games; they are simultaneously excluding the girls and using their knowledge in order to establish mastery of the situation. 'We know something you don't know!' The girls value

far more the cohesive and co-operative relationships they build in the snack bars, as compared with the individualistic and competitive relationships the boys are exhibiting in the arcades.

So it is not just the content of the games that flies in the face of the importance to girls and women of positive social relations; it is also the social context of game-playing that they are likely to find alienating. (So it is not surprising that, in the light of this, girls develop positive attitudes to learning when they are in learning environments that are characterised by co-operative group interaction (Berge 1987) cited by (Clarke and Chambers 1989).)

Playing computer games appears to be part of an initiation process into the wider computer world. If girls find themselves sidelined and unable to participate in this initiation, they will miss what has now become a significant part of the learning process. For instance, not to have participated at this early stage may be one major factor in the low numbers of women studying the subject later in life and taking it up as a career.

## 2.3   Computer Accessibility: Elbows

Computer games are thus a major influence in a world where the vast majority of computers are bought by men. (Celia Hoyles (1988) quotes a BBC survey of 1982 which found that 96% of computer purchasers were men, although as Róisín Ní Mháille Battel (1994) points out, this figure is likely to have dropped by now.) Indeed the home computer tends to be bought for the boy of the family; twice as many boys as girls have access to a computer at home (Straker (1985) and Maurer (1994) list a number of other studies which found this). Lorraine Culley (1986) reports that, whereas 56% of boys said there was a computer at home, this was true of only 22% of girls. In all households with computers boys are 13 times more likely than girls to be using them, and only 4% are used by the mother (EOC 1985).

The dominance of boys in all these aspects of computing is reflected in the fact that purchase of computer magazines is similarly dominated by boys and men. Of three PC magazine offices I contacted (June 1995) at random, one gave a figure of 85% male readership and the other two gave figures of 95% and 97%.

One might think that this imbalance outside the school would be put right to a considerable extent within it. The dismaying thing is that a similar pattern of accessibility seems to hold within the schools, reinforcing the pattern found outside education. I shall be giving a more detailed account of this in Chapter 6 when I discuss secondary education and computing. I shall refer, for example, to the fact that boys make up the vast majority of the members of computer clubs, that when girls try to use computers in out-of-class activities at school, they are elbowed off, that in mixed classes boys hog the best equipment and boys also tend to get more attention from their teachers of computing. School therefore becomes a microcosm of what happens elsewhere, reflecting and reinforcing it rather than correcting it.

## 2.4   Computerphobia?

Given such an onslaught, is it any wonder that many girls react negatively towards computing? Some clearly aren't affected and go on to enjoy a lifetime's work in computing at a high professional level. Others are alienated from the whole area, like some of the girls described by Moore (1986) (and reported by Celia Hoyles): 'at the end of the year the girls felt that they were so far behind that they never wanted a computer in their classroom again.'

Amongst the first to investigate negative reactions was Timothy Jay, who called them computerphobia, a range of resistances, fears, anxieties and hostilities (Jay 1981). These can take such forms as fear of physically touching the computer or of damaging it and what's inside it, a reluctance to read or talk about computers, feeling threatened by those who do know something about them, feeling that you can be replaced by a machine, become a slave to it or feeling aggressive towards computers.

Sanford Weinberg and Mark Fuerst later took up the term 'computerphobia'. They suggested that 5% of people suffer from a severe form of it – so strong a reaction that it involves physical symptoms such as feeling dizzy and faint, and sweating, symptoms commonly associated with panic attacks. On their findings 25% suffer from mild computerphobia, while on the other hand 25% suffer from mild computer*phrenia*, which they define as 'an unrealistically positive attitude towards computer use'. A further 5% suffer from severe computerphrenia, 'an addiction to using computers'. This leaves 40% with 'a normal, balanced attitude towards computer use' (Weinberg and Fuerst 1984, p10).

### Is it the Hardware Alone?

One important question of course is: what exactly is the phobia about? Is it about the hardware – the screen, the keyboard, the box and the noise it all makes? Is it about the hardware plus the software? Or is it about the social context in which the computerphobics expect to have to use the computer? Or, of course, is it a combination of any of these?

Jay certainly includes fear of the computer or fear of damaging it or its contents in some way. While more recently there has been a lot of commentary on how women relate to computer technology as users, there has been very little on how they react to computers as machines. Battel (1994) puts this down to the fact that the commentators who are prepared to talk about technology mainly in terms of physical objects (i.e. machinery) are men who not interested in women's reactions to hardware. Those who are interested in women's reactions, particularly of course feminist writers, resist these narrow definitions of hardware; they insist on definitions of technology that are wider and include what people do with the hardware as well as what they know about it. Donald MacKenzie and Judy Wajcman, for example, state that 'few authors are content with ... a narrow 'hardware' definition of technology ... A computer without programs and programmers is simply a useless collection of bits of metal, plastic and silicon' (MacKenzie and

Wajcman 1985, p3). Therefore these commentators make few observations on women's reaction to the hardware alone.

One example that shows how difficult it is to be sure what people are anxious about is an interview reported by Pamela Kramer and Sheila Lehman. They describe a conversation between a woman, her friend and her husband in which the husband suggests that she is 'bothered by the physical aspects of the thing. The fan. She can't stand the noise the fan makes.' She replies that it's not just that and agrees with her friend that is the discontinuity of the computer with everything else and the fact that it 'forces you to do things its way, and even though it may be faster I don't like it' (Kramer and Lehman 1990, pp65–6).

This idea of computers forcing one to do things their own way links up with an interesting insight of Sherry Turkle's which, although it is not wholly about hardware, nonetheless has a significant input from that direction. Drawing on Karl Marx, she makes the contrast between tools and machines. 'Tools are extensions of their users; machines impose their own rhythm, their rules on the people who work with them . . . ' (Turkle 1984*a*, p172). Lori Nelson, Gine Wiese and Joel Cooper found that people do make a distinction between these two ways of looking at computers and that males and females reacted differently to this distinction. During a period of instruction, females tended to perceive the computer increasingly as a tool, whereas males did not. Moreover females who saw the computers as more of a machine than a tool at the beginning of the study were more likely to drop out than other females. Males, on the other hand, were more likely to stay in the class if they viewed the computer as a machine rather than a tool. They conclude that 'These data indicate that thinking of computers as machines may have detrimental effects on females' affinity for computers. In contrast, it may be beneficial for females to think of computers as tools.' They then add that other research confirms this (Nelson, Wiese and Cooper 1991, p199).

Perhaps enquiry into the feasibility of investigating women's reactions to the hardware has been given up too early. For instance, the phenomenology of viewing the computer as a tool, and therefore as an extension to oneself, or as a constraining machine outside and out of tune with oneself does seem a valuable topic to investigate.

## Negative Reactions

Leaving aside the question of people's reaction to the hardware alone and looking at computing in a broader sense – the hardware plus the software and the social context in which they are used – the subject of negative reactions is widely discussed and researched. In fact it is now a thriving 'sub-industry' amongst academics in some disciplines, for example in psychology and education but surprisingly (or maybe not so surprisingly) not in computer science. However, in spite of the great amount of effort that is being expended in researching this, it remains a quagmire of conflicting results, lack of standardised scales to measure variables and of conceptual disarray. Nonetheless, it is important to attempt to summarise this and to give, where possible, indications of the beginnings of some consensus.

   The term 'computerphobia' is not all that commonly used nowadays; it suggests that all negativity towards computers is fear, begging the question as to whether a distinction should be made between *anxiety* and *attitude*, as more recent researchers have advocated. It seems intuitively obvious that one can have a negative attitude towards computers without being anxious about using them. Heinssen, Glass and Knight suggest that while computer anxiety is 'a function of fear and apprehension, intimidation, hostility and worries that one will be embarrassed, look stupid, or even damage the equipment', computer attitudes have to do with 'feelings about the impact of computers on society and the quality of life . . . ' (Heinssen, Glass and Knight 1987, p50).

   In fact it is not only the relationship between anxiety and attitude that needs to be settled but also the relationship between these and past *experience*, decisions as to how much to work with computers (in the future) and *level of achievement* in using them. There is also *confidence* in using computers and Matthew Maurer (1994), in a review of factors whose relationship with computer anxiety has been investigated, adds *gender*, *age*, *personality traits* and so-called *math anxiety* to this list. Igbaria, Schiffman and Wieckowski (1994) add *perceived usefulness* and *perceived fun*.

   One question where there is surely no need to take sides is whether anxiety determines experience which, in turn, determines achievement or, on the contrary, whether it is level of experience that determines the level of anxiety and this determines the level of achievement.

   There is likely to be a two-way causality between these elements. This is suggested in Figure 2.1 where attitude is also included as an important variable. For instance, level of anxiety can influence level of experience; a student anxious about using computers is less likely to join computer clubs or voluntarily enrol on computer courses. This will lead to a greater feeling of anxiety. Conversely, experience (of the right sort) can reduce anxiety and this in turn will lead to seeking further experience. The operation of two-way causality is indeed likely to set up virtuous or vicious spirals upwards or downwards. Someone who has the experience needed to counteract anxiety will not only seek yet more experience, he or she will also achieve more, raising further his or her level of experience and lowering further his or her level of anxiety and so on. On the other hand, people so anxious that they evade experience will increase their anxiety, further decreasing their experience and their achievement, adding yet further to their anxiety.

   The relationship between attitude and anxiety is probably more problematic. A lot obviously depends on how 'attitude' is defined. If 'attitude' is defined in terms of the individual's view of whether computers will benefit society or not, a person with a favourable attitude towards computing on this definition could have a high, or a low, level of anxiety about engaging in computing themselves. In just the same way a person may have a positive attitude towards the benefits of surgery but a very high anxiety level if they themselves had to act as surgeons.

   On the other hand some researchers have chosen to include in their definition of 'computer attitude' three subscales: computer liking, computer confidence and computer anxiety.

   A more substantial source of contention is whether the anxiety/attitude/

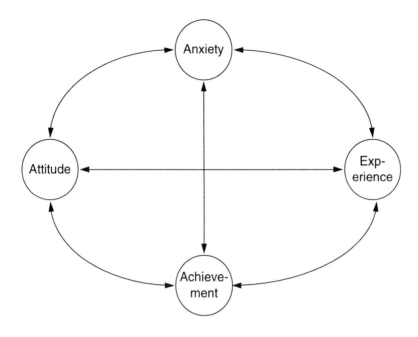

**Figure 2.1:** *Influences on Computer Anxiety*

experience mixture leads to different levels of achievement or whether what it leads to is choosing, or not choosing, whether to opt for more involvement with computing or less. When females do take part in computer programming courses it has been found that they do as well as, or better than, the males and are disproportionately highly represented among successful students (Mandinach and Linn 1987).

## 2.5   The Plot Thickens . . .

It is tempting to think that those who stand to benefit from a large scale social process, consciously and intentionally contribute towards that process. This is often a mistake. People can bring about social change as the result of lots of uncoordinated individual actions, the conscious motives for which simply don't include the effect which does in fact result. For instance, a lot of individual house buyers in a situation where houses are scarce will raise the general level of house prices by offering that little bit more in order to get the particular house they want for their immediate family. Clearly it would be absurd to think in terms of conspiracies in these cases.

The fact remains that it looks as if large scale unemployment together with a great deal of underemployment is here to stay. Indeed it is here to grow. Large scale structural changes are taking place simultaneously with relatively minor booms and slumps. For instance, whole layers of middle management are being 'stripped out' in quite a few industries. This of course is largely made possible by the introduction of powerful information technology which can do the jobs that people did before – and more besides. As more and more people find themselves unemployed, or underemployed, one of the safest places to be employed is in the information technology industry which is facilitating the reduction in jobs.

And of course it is not just a matter of jobs, it is also about power. If the dominant social group is to keep and extend its power during an information revolution, then clearly it must control the information technology underlying it.

Again, I am not suggesting that men have consciously set out to dominate computing with these objectives of maintaining their own employment and power during a period of increasing unemployment and the increasingly pivotal role of information technology. The job-gendering of computing was taking place long before the information revolution and structural unemployment could have been predicted. In any case, the masculinisation of computing, at any rate at the higher levels, is simply par for the course and what men would do with any roles which carry kudos. But the new situation, which has only just started, is providing further strong motives for this masculinisation of computing and for resisting the 'encroachment' of women.

What better way of doing this could there be than not only convincing boys and men that the higher reaches of computing are their preserve, but also convincing the girls and women that this is so? In their study of tertiary students in Australia, Clarke and Chambers asked their subjects to rate 12 computer-related occupations as male or female activities. The men rated three occupations as more suitable for women (data entry, primary school computing teacher and computer operator) and seven in varying degrees as more suitable for men than for women (computer programmer, secondary school computing teacher, computing lecturer, systems analyst, computer salesperson, professor of computing and computer centre manager). The women, on the other hand, rated fewer jobs as being suitable for one gender rather than the other. Significantly, they agreed with the men in rating two jobs as being more appropriate for women (data entry and primary school computing teacher), jobs which conventionally are relatively low in status. Equally significantly, they agreed with the men in rating five high status jobs as being more suitable for men (computing tutor, computing lecturer, computer salesperson, professor of computing and computer centre manager) (Clarke and Chambers 1989, pp418–19).

Clearly a person's perception of an activity as not suitable to her or his gender will have a considerable influence on which jobs that person applies for or seeks prior training in. Girls therefore are much more likely to self-select themselves into 'lower status' jobs and select themselves out of the 'higher status' jobs – boys are obviously going to do the reverse and select themselves into the 'higher status' jobs, spurning the data entry clerks' positions.

A feature that is likely to exacerbate the tendency of women to select themselves out of the 'higher status' jobs in computing is the 'we can, I can't' paradox in which women find themselves (Francis 1994, p285). This is the belief that, while women as a whole are as good as men, the same individuals who believe this could each think of themselves as less able than men. So a woman might believe that women should hold an equal number of 'high status' jobs as men, but be very unlikely to think of applying for such posts herself.

The forces working against women applying for these jobs are extremely powerful. How else could it be that these jobs are, for reasons I have just discussed, 'the ones to go for' and yet, as we shall see in Chapter 6, women are voting with their feet, and minds, against undergraduate computing courses? I shall go in greater depth into the mutually reinforcing influences that produce this effect. One of these is the home, the subject of the next chapter.

# 3

# And Not in the Home

*I believe that [women's] disabilities elsewhere are only clung to in order to maintain their subordination in domestic life; because the generality of the male sex cannot yet tolerate the idea of living with an equal.* John Stuart Mill 1869 (Mill 1984, p299)

## 3.1   What is to be Cinderella's Fate?

Housework has been, and is only too likely to remain, the Cinderella of the technological era, the victim of men's devaluation of such work combined with their continuing appropriation of technology. For a start, most household technology introduced since the industrial revolution has been the result of the development of equipment for use outside the home and only introduced there as an afterthought.

Secondly, this development is controlled by men, and its introduction into the home for housework does not occur until retention of this control is ensured through maintenance procedures and planned obsolescence. Of course, profits play a part here, but this explanation is at the more conscious and, in a sense, at the more respectable end of the range. What I mean can perhaps be shown by taking the parallel of men dominating the workplace. Here, obviously, getting bigger salaries has something to do with it, but there is another and less conscious motivation which is at least as powerful. As Mill suggests in the quotation heading this chapter, dominating the workplace is done mainly so that men can avoid admitting that their partners at home are equal. And of course power means more to many than a high income. So controlling the introduction of technology into the home is not just about profits, but also about power and dominance.

The third point about the introduction of technology into the home is that, more often than not, it is a mixed blessing. A new piece of equipment will not necessarily save time – time spent assembling and cleaning it can outstrip the time saved in operating it. Moreover the time saved rarely, in itself, leaves the houseworker free to do other things; this time is instead used in the pursuit of higher standards.

Cinderella will remain Cinderella in spite of the introduction of information technology while she continues to await 'rescue' by her handsome prince. Women's position in relation to men has not been improved by what has taken place at a low-tech level and will only be repeated at a high-tech level unless women take an alternative view of computers, and computers in housework. They, as the majority of household workers, will have to take control of computers. In this chapter I shall examine just how slow has been the introduction of computers into the household for housework, and I shall suggest some ways in which they could be used. But the overriding message must be that unless women gain control of this technology and thereby empower themselves, they will end up suffering one or other of Cinderella's fates – condemned either to the kitchen or to some sort of gilded cage.

I say that women should gain control of household technology but, of course, ideally this would only be an interim measure. As I explained in the first chapter, I do not believe that jobs are inherently more suited to one gender than another, nor is a particular gender inherently suited to one set of jobs rather than another. People should be free to take up the work that best suits them as individuals and this will mean that many women will not wish to do housework and many men will find the job extremely satisfying. Whoever does the job should have control over the development of the technology needed for it.

## 3.2 The Trivialisation of Women's Work

For the foreseeable future it looks as if women will be doing virtually all the housework. Moreover it sometimes seems as if it were a 'Law of Nature' that whatever women work at, men seek to devalue and whatever is devalued men leave women to work at. We shall see this in the computing workplace, a microcosm that reflects a much wider phenomenon. For example, the most common type of work done by women is housework to which no monetary value is attached and which, moreover, never features in the calculation of any nation's Gross Domestic Product. It is difficult to grasp the enormity of omitting the contribution of this gigantic service industry, 'employing' as it does half the adult population. In spite of, as we shall see, the diversity of skills and managerial expertise involved in housework, men still see it as 'mere housework' and unintelligent.

### 'I Don't Work – I'm Only a Housewife'

Not regarding housework as productive in the economic sense only strengthens this demeaning view. It is frequently observed that one effect of industrialisation was the change from households being units of both production and consumption to being units of consumption only. Prior to the industrial revolution householders kept their own animals for consumption, grew their own wheat, collected their own fuel and so on. Subsequently these commodities were available for purchase and in terms of effort and cost it made little sense for householders to produce these consumables themselves. In this respect houseworkers did become consumers only. But this categorisation ignores all the other work – cooking, cleaning, child care – that still occurs in the household. In these respects houseworkers are clearly producers; they are producers as skilled manual workers and as service workers and managers. The failure to acknowledge this contribution to the economy and to persist in labelling housewives as 'consumers' only serves to reinforce the perceived triviality of housework.

Another significant effect of industrialisation was the development of the 'doctrine of separate spheres'. On the one hand there is the place of work, until recently predominantly inhabited by men and most certainly still controlled by men, and on the other hand, the place of rest or home, maintained by women for men and the remainder of the family (Schwartz Cowan 1983, p18).

The word 'home' conjures up images of a place of rest and succour – 'home-sweet-home'. These images tend to mask the many forms of work that occur there. It is normal, for instance, even for housewives, to contrast 'being at work' with 'being at home', as if home did not involve work. But there is a great deal of work to be performed there if it is to be maintained as a sanctuary, a place of succour and a unit for raising children.

As a sanctuary, home provides for its occupants relaxation, shelter, recreation, food and clothing for which both manual and managerial work is needed. In the majority of contemporary western households manual work is required in the form of shopping (including travelling to the shops and transporting purchases back to the home), cooking, washing (normally in washing machines located in the home), ironing, vacuuming, dusting and other forms of cleaning. Young children also require manual work for their upbringing: the preparation of food, feeding, nursing, changing clothes, teaching basic skills like feeding themselves, learning to walk; they also have to be transported. Managerial work occurs in the home in the form of overseeing children and teenagers, keeping household accounts, paying bills on time, arranging for visits from maintenance people to maintain and sometimes clean equipment. Elderly relatives either require manual work, overseeing or both. And so on – and on.

And, of course, this blend of manual and managerial tasks, with the high level of responsibility involved, continues for the housewife long after the 'breadwinner' has returned home from his 'hard day at work' – just as it usually starts even before he sets out.

## Traditional Household Technology

What technology is available to assist in all this housework? (The word 'housework' does at least acknowledge that the home involves work.) Not surprisingly, in the light of the downgrading of work in the home, very little of the technology introduced in this and the last century that we use for manual or managerial work in our homes was developed originally for housework. Much of it was first invented for other purposes, mainly industrial and commercial: refrigerators, carpet sweepers, vacuum cleaners, dishwashers, non-stick frying pans, sewing machines – even, in the US, piped water and sewerage. And the magnetron, used for military purposes for improved radar equipment in 1940, was subsequently converted for heating and the microwave oven.

This derivative nature of household technology is not surprising given the undervaluation of housework. These machines are often considered to be a luxury that men and women are encouraged to buy as a treat for the housewife and to save her time.

But what has been the impact of this second-hand technology on the life of the housewife – how much time has it actually saved her? On the face of it, a washing machine does save time and drudgery, modern central heating systems likewise, in obvious ways. But looked at more closely the overall impact on the life of the housewife has been negligible. Ruth Schwartz Cowan quotes some remarkable statistics from the US. A large national sample collected in 1965 showed that the time the average American woman spent doing housework and caring for children was not strikingly different from the time spent by affluent housewives in 1912 (Schwartz Cowan 1983, p199). And other surveys show that the total time spent on housework by women not employed outside the home was about 52 hours per week in 1924 rising to 55 hours per week in the 1960s (Vanek 1974). And a UK report published in 1993 cites a figure of at least 80 hours of unpaid work being done by half of the women who work full-time at home (Butler 1993).

Two factors seem to have been at work in perpetuating this workload. One is that the introduction of technology in the first part of the twentieth century coincided with fewer people being available to work in the household. Men left to work outside the home and fewer servants were available because of war and other factors. The new technology may have made individual tasks easier but now the housewife had to do them all.

The second factor has been that whatever time technology has saved over and above making up for fewer servants has, in practice, been filled by the pursuit of pointlessly higher standards of cleanliness and purity. More often than not the housewife is expected to use this 'liberated' time for yet more housework; standards simply become more stringent – more clothes get washed, floors are cleaned more frequently, cooking procedures become even more complex. Instead of freeing her to do things other than housework, this technology all too often facilitates what Cowan so eloquently describes as 'the senseless tyranny of spotless shirts and polished floors' (Schwartz Cowan 1983, p216); to which must be added the futility of endless ironing.

The telephone provides yet another example of a common household appliance developed first as a business 'tool' to replicate the telegraph. It was subsequently used in the home for sending messages, for ordering goods, in medical care, assisting in organising children's education and many other purposes.

But, of course, while its use does save time like other household appliances, it has always had considerable social uses. These were resisted by the telephone industry in the United States which condemned them as what one manager called in 1909 'purely idle gossip'. (This is at least partly explained by early US pricing policies: only an annual flat fee for the line was charged, all calls were then free within the exchange area.) He sought to reduce this 'unnecessary use' (Fischer 1988, p48).

These are social uses, not uses for housework as such. But these social uses are valuable and include not just 'purely idle gossip' but, for example, interaction over a distance between an otherwise scattered family. In this respect it is rather like the conversations of the girls at the edge of the playground which I discussed in Chapter 2. The girls themselves demurely said they were 'just talking'; in fact they were discussing what were often quite important issues in their families. In the same way this 'purely idle gossip' is important in reducing women's isolation while they work at home – though one has to treat this with some caution: without some more basic change in conditions, this social use could be merely a garland of flowers over the chains.

### 'White Goods' and 'Brown Goods'

In modern studies of household technology the distinction is often made between 'white goods' and 'brown goods'. White goods are such things as conventional ovens, automatic toasters, refrigerators that are generally sold to women; some of these are often decorated with motifs thought to appeal to women. Brown goods on the other hand are hi-fi equipment, radios, televisions, camcorders and so on. These are generally marketed for men and their colour, while not necessarily brown, is not white; indeed they are usually black. These 'masculine' goods are for hobbies and entertainment and are perceived as gadgets, whereas white goods, in spite of their sometimes fancy exteriors, are for everyday domestic work.

Attitudes to some items of domestic technology can be ambivalent however. Cynthia Cockburn and Susan Ormrod in a study of the microwave oven describe how one retail firm had two distinct types of shop: one selling brown goods to men and the other selling white goods to families (Cockburn and Ormrod 1993). In this firm, the microwave oven started life in the brown goods chain of shops, where it was sold as a gadget – a 'Piewarmer'. Subsequently it was moved to the white goods chain to be sold for serious cookery and 'real' housework; this was for a number of reasons, the main one being that it was no longer a technical novelty.

## 3.3   Uses for Computers in the Home

### Present Uses

Major uses of computer technology in the home are for recreational purposes and social communication and not for housework. The applications of microcomputers and microchips which first spring to mind are in computer games, videos and televisions. Next comes the personal computer used for playing games and for wordprocessing. As a wordprocessor it is often kept in a room designated as an office and admittedly sometimes used for writing letters and other documents as part of the managerial activity of the home.

Turning to housework, microchips are built into devices like washing machines, dishwashers, microwave ovens and central heating controls. These devices only require simple manipulation to operate them: turning a dial, pressing switches and it surely won't be all that long before they react to voice; they do not require the operation of a keyboard or comparable input device. These machines have a selection of programs from which the operator can choose. The more advanced sewing and knitting machines have connections to PCs which enable the user to create her or his own designs. These designs can then be 'downloaded' onto the sewing or knitting machines and these will then automatically stitch or knit the designs and motifs.

Many electrical household appliances are now enhanced by the use of 'fuzzy logic' in programs incorporated in their microchips. Computer hardware operates using a binary system: everything is either 0 or 1; switches are either on or off; statements are true or not true; a person is either adult or not adult, there are no other possible values – no in-between values. Fuzzy logic, on the other hand, admits the possibility of many values of 'adulthoodness'. Fuzzy logic is therefore a multivalued logic as distinct from the traditional two-valued, or binary, logic.

Fuzzy logic also has another meaning: reasoning about 'fuzzy sets'. An example of a fuzzy set is the set of all adults. We do not know exactly what defines an adult, therefore we do not know exactly which individuals are the members of this set. Similarly we do not know exactly what is chilly and what is cold. Fuzzy logic in this second sense allows us to say that at a certain temperature a room is, for example, both chilly *and* cold. And a central heating system that is controlled by a microchip programmed with 'fuzzy logic' will fire off the boiler to warm up the room not at full blast but at a speed that reflects the ambivalence of the definition of the temperature. Fuzzy rules can be finely tuned so that the heating reacts sensitively and doesn't overshoot and overheat, or undershoot and leave the room too cold.

There are washing machines whose microchips are programmed to store fuzzy rules that can regulate the washing cycle according to the load and type of stains. Fuzzy programming in micro-wave ovens can continuously measure temperature, humidity and changes in the shape of food and adjust cooking patterns accordingly. Fuzzy logic is used in modern vacuum cleaners (adjusting to dust quantity and floor type), clothes driers (adjusting drying time and temperature to load and fabric type), dishwashers (adjusting washing strategy according to the number of dishes and the type of food left on the dishes), rice cookers (adjusting to rice volume and current temperature) and refrigerators (setting defrosting times and frequency according to usage) (Kosko 1994). These extra facilities often make little substantial difference to the labour involved, they merely alter the 'feel' of the work.

Shopping from home using telecommunications has been available for a decade. By subscribing to a videotex[1] service such as British Telecom's PRESTEL, users have access to an information service and can place orders for goods using a keypad. While the information services provided by these videotex systems proved quite popular, the teleshopping and telebanking services had only limited success in the UK (Miles 1988, p113), though teleshopping is very popular in the US. Current research is aimed at providing customers with user-helpful sales service: pictures of

---

[1] *Videotex* is a generic name for the technologies required to provide textual information for display on a screen. It incorporates *teletext* and *viewdata*.

goods, automatic debiting facilities, delivery services and even a complaints hot-line where customers can show faulty goods to a retailer over a video-link. Where these facilities are taking off and becoming the norm, they would seem likely to encourage houseworkers to remain in their houses and to increase the isolation of those who already have little opportunity for social contact.

## Why So Few Computers?

We have already seen how domestic work is not considered *real* work. The doctrine of separate spheres reinforces this idea – real work takes place outside the home. The payoff from this for men has three components. First, this attitude ensures that men and children can be nourished and maintained at no monetary cost for the labour involved. Secondly, if one class of person can be retained to do this job for no pay it ensures the economic dominance of the class that is paid for its *real* work. Thirdly, and the reason we are interested in this now is that, given that the home cannot be a producer of monetary wealth, there is no paramount need to develop technology for domestic use *per se*. These three factors mean that women lack the purchasing power that would give them effective demand for well designed domestic appliances. If men did the housework and hence it was considered real work, and if, as a result, they earned disposable income from it, then there would be a huge market for sophisticated domestic equipment.

We have also seen how technology is introduced into the home after it has been developed elsewhere and for other purposes. Technological devices arrive in the home after their initial design is established by men, and women have little or no control over subsequent changes in design. Moreover, these devices arrive only after maintenance procedures have been set up, procedures in which women are not involved – maintenance engineers are rarely female. In the household women have to take what they are given. It is my belief that the comparative scarcity of computers in the home as compared with the office for example, and the tardiness of their arrival in the home (apart from use by men and boys) is due to the fact that men are still in the process of establishing control of this form of technology. Judging by earlier instances of the introduction of household technology, only when this control is firmly established and patterns of use and maintenance are fully set will computers appear in the home on any scale.

Male control of the introduction of computer technology into the home is reinforced not just by trivialising it, but by making it an object of ridicule. I remember an applicant for the post of lecturer in Computer Science who, on being asked to what uses his research had been put, replied 'washing machines' – to laughter from almost everybody present. It was a joke.

Usually the application of computers in the domestic setting is just not considered. When I mentioned the possibility of greater use of computers in the home, a colleague asked 'What would you use them for?' It seems strange that somebody whose working life requires him to teach others to use computers in their work, who spends a high proportion of that time working on techniques and methods that will be used for production, appears *never* to have applied his mind to enhancing domestic work with computers.

The literature on this subject both reflects and reinforces these views. If we look at books from the 1970s and 1980s on computers and society, some never mention domestic applications for computers at all. In a book entitled *Computers in Society* (Sanders 1973), for example, the chapters concerned with applications which directly affect the individual have titles such as Individuals and Computers, Computers and Health, Computers and Medicine, Computers in Education. Private individuals gain (or otherwise) from the utilisation of computers because of their use in the public sphere, in schools, in hospitals – incredibly there is no discussion of their use in the home.

Moving on to 1980, Murray Laver's *Computers and Social Change* (Laver 1980) includes an imaginative chapter entitled 'The Domesticated Computer'. In this he accurately forecasts telephonic facilities much as we have them today, indeed British Telecom's research programme for the 'Home of the Future' incorporates some of the innovations he suggests. Murray Laver anticipates more sophisticated washing machines which adjust wash cycles to different weights and mixes of fabric; advanced cooking machines with automatic hoppers and security systems are amongst his other proposals. (I did not find any references to voice activated domestic appliances in this book, but these would seem very much in line with his suggestions.)

Murray Laver outlines facilities for telecommuting (working from home on a computer connected to the office) to enable ('married') women to work part-time from home when their children are young. The conclusion to this chapter reads

> Clearly, computer assisted automation is potentially as pervasive and powerful an influence in the home as it is at work, and we might end by relieving men and women of much routine activity ... The combination of microcomputer control with electric motor driving power could indeed emancipate us from the slavery of domestic routine. In doing so it would, however, add to the 'burden' of leisure, and some of us may decide to continue to exercise our muscles and relax our minds as we busy ourselves with undemanding chores ...
>
> [So] of course, it by no means follows that everything that is technically feasible will be done. Although strong commercial interests will seek to exploit the burgeoning capacity of the microelectronics industry, much will depend on the general economic situation, on the attitudes of society to what some may see as a 'frivolous' use of scarce resources, and on the common sense and sales resistance of individual customers (Laver 1980, pp67–86).

On the whole Murray Laver is on the side of the angels; he acknowledges the importance of those who would benefit from technology having control over it. His quotation marks around the word 'frivolous' support this; while many may consider such applications frivolous, the author does not.

He does, however, to some extent compromise this message with his idea that we may need to retain some of the more routine tasks and 'undemanding chores'.

One can see some force in his idea that common sense may well resist the buying of all possible gadgets. Who wants a computer controlled tin-opener because that's all a husband can think of to buy his wife for Christmas? But one suspects this came from a man for whom these tedious household tasks are in fact not routine, from somebody who wants relief from the taxing demands of 'real' work elsewhere. It did not come from somebody who bears the responsibility of ensuring that all this housework is done and whose job is entirely taken up with this 'slavery'.

In a later book, *Home Informatics*, Ian Miles (1988) gives a more far-reaching examination of modern household technology. But, even here, the word 'formal' is used to describe paid work based outside the home and 'informal' to describe unpaid work carried out inside the home.

Technological descriptions of an impressive range of Home Informatics (HI) and their uses are covered. The emphasis is on communications: all forms of television, video, interpersonal communications. Electronic technology for housework is examined, but not to the same extent as technology for leisure activities. Ian Miles observes what we have commented on earlier, namely that the availability of Home Informatics products is the result of research and development 'based on perceptions of the industrial market rather than the consumer market' and that 'much consumer technology is the result of technological transfer from the formal economy'.[2]

Ian Miles' assertion here is that Home Informatics is seen as peripheral to the important areas of advanced IT only because of 'scepticism and snobbery' (p47). This is a crucial point and the question arises: whose scepticism and snobbery? It is not the consumers who adopt a snobbish approach; it is the high-tech enthusiasts who automatically consider that IT in the sphere of Home Informatics is not at the cutting-edge, whereas most other commercial and military applications are. How could something so trivial as housework possibly be at the forefront of technology? But it is these high-tech enthusiasts who are, in fact, in control. Is it any wonder then that there is little or no development of computers for the home?

Having identified the central issue Ian Miles, like Murray Laver, then strangely (or is it so strange?) backtracks by saying that

> Possibly the real obstacle to such erstwhile IT enthusiasts taking HI
> seriously is really that the latter are unsettled by the rather more
> competitive market for consumer equipment than for, say, missile
> guidance systems! (p4)

Since when have entrepreneurs avoided competition in the arms market or been reluctant to compete in selling detergents, washing machines or vacuum cleaners? The reason, as I have argued and as Ian Miles himself sees, lies elsewhere.

By 1993 the picture had not changed. This typical lack of momentum was highlighted by a BBC2 *Horizon* programme *The Electronic Frontier* (*Horizon* 1993) in which much was made of the idea that introducing the computer into the workplace was only half the job. The other half – that of introducing computers into the home – had yet to be done. Spokesmen from the information industry made it sound almost

---

[2] Note again the idea that the houseworker is merely a consumer not a producer (see page 28).

as if this burden was being shouldered out of altruism; what they did not say was that, having saturated the workplace with computers, they now had to find new markets. Turning to the home was a desperate second phase forced upon them.

Once again the same old story is reflected in the tasks the home-based computers were to facilitate. These were imaginative and futuristic, especially in the areas of information and communication; they included the idea of digitising a million paintings, photographs and images of all sorts. Another example was having any book or text available in written prose, sound or video. But there was nothing to do with domestic work: nothing about child care, shopping, cleaning, maintenance, household accounts, cooking, family diaries – in short, not a single mention of what we know as housework; far less in fact than the two earlier books we have just discussed. Indeed according to Bill Gates,[3] 'At home you want to relax, you want to be entertained . . . '

And again in 1993 the *Independent on Sunday* presented this same point neatly packaged in a short article about British Telecom's (BT's) research programme 'Home of the Future' (*Independent on Sunday* 7 December 1993, p12). The man interviewed to describe this 'new' vision of the home is Professor Cochrane, research manager at BT. We are told how he too envisages a 'vast smorgasbord of video, text, data, graphics, cinema-quality sound, and even virtual reality to be fed straight into the home via the telephone network.' There is little reference to all the work that goes on in the home. Electronic gadgetry will be linked to an electronic butler whom you can phone and instruct to turn things on. If you see a wok in a cookery programme, you can turn to the video-shopping channel to order one. The article ends with a glimpse of the professor's domestic life: 'Somehow the professor still finds energy at the end of the week for mind-stretching projects with his four children. He recently taught one of his young sons about lift and drag on an aircraft by building a 'wind tunnel' with his wife's decidedly old-tech hair-drier.' Somehow the 'wind of change' seems to be passing her by.

*Plus ça change, plus c'est la même chose.*

## 3.4 Computers and Real Housework

We have seen how the present number of uses for computers in the home is very small. It is impossible to foresee all of the developments that will take place, but I would like to sketch a selection of further uses. It must be emphasised, however, that it should be women who are empowered to make the final choice, including choosing from the technologies already available outside the home for introduction into it. And, most importantly, they should also be empowered to control the development of technology designed for the home in the first place.

So, first let us look at how we could use technology that is already available but, so far, largely only outside the home.

---

[3] Bill Gates is the Chairman and Chief Executive of Microsoft Corporation, presently the world's largest software company; he is the instigator of many important software innovations.

## Bytes

As someone who has to use recipes to prepare interesting meals, my first interest is in making recipes easier to access. The idea of women using computers for recipes is not new (Rothschild 1983, p89) and recently a series of software packages entitled *Cookbook* has appeared on the market (Lifestyle Software Group n.d.); Mrs Beeton too is now presented in this form. This must be new to by far the majority of women, so I would like to sketch such an up-to-date system, one which largely but not entirely overlaps with the *Cookbook* series and which I shall call *Bytes*.

*Bytes* requires a computer that does not have to be in the kitchen itself although the slimline monitor and adapted 'mouse', or some other form of user interface, obviously have to be. Whatever device is used to communicate with the computer, let us assume that it's protected from food and water.

*Bytes* has a good indexing system to a large database of recipes. Having located a recipe I want, I can have a colour picture displayed on the monitor to show me what the results of my labour should look like. Indeed I can have windows, small sections of the larger screen, in which are shown videos of someone making the dish. There is also a device on the side of the machine that I can simply touch in order to have any of the steps in the recipe output in sound, so I only have to listen – I don't have to read the recipe whilst cooking. I have seven people to feed and not four, which is the number all my old recipe books cater for. The adjustments up and down for more or fewer people may well not be linear, that is, you may not require twice as much of every ingredient for twice as many people, or a quarter of each of the ingredients if you are cooking only for one. *Bytes* has a facility that allows me to specify the number of people to be fed as a parameter, so the quantities of each ingredient for seven people are automatically calculated.

If it's a dish, like a soufflé which, if doubled, would require two dishes for cooking rather than simply providing a dish twice as large, *Bytes* tells me what dishes I need. If it were a matter of a larger dish, it is unlikely to take twice as long to cook – *Bytes* tells me how long it will take. Some of my friends have ranges (Aga's for example) for which the cooking times are quite different from those for conventional gas or electric ovens – again a parameter supplied at set-up time would ensure that all recipes are presented for cooking on the type of stove specified; *Bytes* adapts instructions for microwave ovens as well.

If a complex recipe requires a more basic recipe like shortcrust pastry or béchamel sauce and I choose not to buy these ready made, then these sub-recipes can be 'popped-up' in windows. A glossary that explains basic terms to the novice cook is provided by means of a 'help' facility.

If I particularly like a recipe, I can mark it for future reference. *Bytes* has a facility for recording notes about adjustments I have made to suit my own tastes.

For those with dietary restrictions the benefits are obvious. For example, I can if I wish select only those recipes that are gluten or sugar free. Two of my children are vegetarians; when they come to stay I search *Bytes* for vegetarian food.

When I come home from work tired in the evening and have only pork and potatoes available left over from the previous day, I can get, within seconds, a selection of recipes that use these as their main ingredients. *Bytes* has a facility that allows me to record the basic ingredients (flour, sugar, spices, etc.) with a long shelf life which I normally stock in my larder. So, a further requirement for these recipes is that, not only must the recipes use pork and potatoes, but only the basic ingredients I have recorded earlier.

If I pay a subscription to the publishers of *Bytes* they will send me regular updates with new recipes that are posted to me on a floppy disk. I can also make one-off payments for a disk on say Indian or Italian cookery.

### Is this feasible?

Of course it is. The wonder is it has taken so long.

For some years now most of the commonly used database management packages have been capable of holding a database of recipes, providing index facilities and allowing updates in the form of notes and markers. I have already implied that problems with conventional hardware, using a keyboard or a mouse in a kitchen environment and so on could be overcome – a touchscreen is one possibility. If it is possible to design an input device for use in a dirty industrial environment or a pub, it is surely not difficult to design one for kitchen use.

These recipe packages have long been overdue and, even so, it is doubtful if many women know of their existence. Of those who do know about them – perhaps their partners have bought them one as a Christmas present – few will have all the hardware necessary and in the right place for really effective use (suitable input device, monitor appropriately positioned with all the wiring this involves, etc.).

The cost of providing this in its entirety is fairly high if measured by the cost of other domestic technology. But it would not be nearly as much as the cost of installing central heating or building a conservatory. It would probably cost no more than the extra many families are happy to spend on additional comfort, gadgetry and status symbolism in their cars. Yet it is possible to speculate that only a handful of women in the country have such a system fully installed.

## Medical Diagnosis

The 1970s saw the development of *expert systems*. These are programs for performing tasks that require expertise but no great insight. A number were developed for medical diagnosis for use by physicians. The expert system, or program, asks the operator or physician questions about the background of the patient: age and sex. Questions about symptoms are then presented one at a time; the way in which the questioning will proceed depends on the answers given at each step. The expert system eventually comes up with a diagnosis (or, with some programs, multiple diagnoses) and even offers suggestions for drug treatment.

For a number of reasons these never entered general use – not least because they came up with some rather bizarre diagnoses and were cumbersome for a physician to use. It is true that the state of the art has improved since the 1970s and wholly new software and hardware techniques are being utilised to solve these problems.

But why is it that nobody has ever, to my knowledge, developed a marketable scaled down version of these programs for parents with sick children? There may be possible legal issues here if parents are for instance misled by what an expert system advises. But many of us made extensive use of Dr Spock in the '60s and '70s trying to distinguish between measles, german measles and chickenpox. All that was needed was something with more detail than Spock and his successors provided and, above all, some pictures – of spots! Better still would be some videos with sound to show not just the spots but the way children move and cough, etc. when they are sick.

These systems need not be confined to children's ailments. They could of course apply to adults and indeed to the veterinary sphere of pets and other domestic animals.

But, of course, to have developed this software in this way would be to have followed the classic pattern of developing it first for the 'professionals' and subsequently for the housewife. Moreover and, in the wider sense, more seriously, these ideas will not save the housewife much time. They will enhance her work in much the same way that a wordprocessor or an electronic diary enhances the work of a secretary.

## Computer Networks within the Home

There are initiatives that offer a range of telecommunication computing services and IT training to women and men who have not had the opportunity to acquire this type of skill. Two of these launched in the UK are the Manchester based Electronic Village Halls (EVH) and TeleCottages Wales. These are centres outside the home, but close to it, where people can drop in and use computer packages and electronic mail. If they don't know how to use these, then facilities are provided for learning. Known by other names such as Community Computer Centres and Telework Centres, they are local initiatives for both urban and rural communities. A café in central London called Cyberia Café intends to train people (mainly women) in the same sort of way but including new uses of the Internet, which I shall describe shortly.

But these are still *outside* the home, not *inside* it. Moreover, the way these services are offered implies, 'It's very easy, even you can do it'. This is undoubtedly a first step towards overcoming women's fear of machines and their lack of confidence, but it is nonetheless patronising; women are using computers under a protective patriarchal arm and overseeing eye.

None of these facilities make use of software or hardware developed expressly for domestic use. Just as with earlier domestic technologies of the nineteenth and twentieth centuries which are nearly all by-products of the commercial and industrial world, so these technologies which are now coming near to (not into) the domestic scene are spin-offs from developments for other spheres of interest. As I just noted, even my proposals for recipes and medical advice systems would utilise existing software, and would not call for new, technology.

So far I have implied, by not suggesting any alternative, that a computer running *Bytes* would stand alone in the household and would be in or near the kitchen. It

would not be connected to any other computers in the household nor indeed to the outside world.

But what if we provided a network within the household so that a parent could, while working in the kitchen, monitor electronically and thus 'view' what her or his children were doing on the PC in their bedroom?[4] While this would raise quite valid issues about prying on one's children, it should at least be an option in the debate about children's use of computers at home and the deleterious effects of this. Moreover there are, as we shall shortly see, considerable advantages in linking the home PC to the outside world. For instance, in the case of *Bytes*, rather than having separate copies in each PC, there could be a central copy to which users subscribe and access over a national network. Updates and corrections would be made centrally and thus there would be no need to send out individual floppy discs with new recipes. Users' personal notes could still be held locally on the home PC, and they could make electronic copies of any recipes they fancied.

If women had more control of the use of computers in the household and were seen to be competent at this, then both girls and boys would have a wholly different view of what women were capable of. Women would set the system up, determine who would have access to what software and when they could use it. If women were known to have computing skills, then a young lad with a computer in his bedroom would not assume that he could outwit his mother.

## Computer Networks Linking Home to the Outside World

At work an increasing number of people now communicate with one another via electronic mail, or 'e-mail', as well as by telephone, not just within their own organisations but also with people outside. This is achieved via the Internet , a huge world-wide computer network linking smaller networks through a giant mass of cables, other telecommunication links and computers. For instance, the computer in my office is linked into one of the smaller networks, JANET, which stands for Joint Academic Network, just one of the many networks forming the Internet. Currently, in late 1995, the Internet links over two million computers and users are estimated at more than 44 million – this last figure represents a spectacular increase of 25% over the last 12 months.

The Internet, incidentally, exists because, in the early 1970s, the US military was fearful that a central control centre could be knocked out in a military attack. Communications would then be impossible. An international network ensures alternative routes for communications. It was not originally intended for what has now become one of its major uses – personal communication on any subject. It can be readily introduced into the home. All the hardware that is needed is a telephone line, a relatively inexpensive modem and a PC. This is no harder to set up than installing a video recorder, but the knowledge of how to do it is less readily available to those outside the appropriate technical sphere. Moreover, the cost of accessing the Internet is extremely high for most home users. Nevertheless, if it were to be

---

[4] Ian Miles suggests the name 'homenet' for a network that would link household devices within households paralleling Local Area Networks linking users within one business organisation (Miles 1988, p33).

introduced on a large scale into the home, it would, like all the other technology I have mentioned, have been developed first and foremost for other purposes.

As well as enabling one-to-one and one-to-many correspondence – you can send messages to several people simultaneously – these networks support 'e-mail lists' or special interest groups which computer users can join. Messages put out by any member of the list are automatically sent to you once you are a member. And you can contribute too. Slightly different from these e-mail lists are 'newsgroups' to which anyone can contribute, but you have to take the initiative to read it; the information isn't automatically sent to you. No one body owns Internet and any control of what is passed over the electronic links has to be instituted by senders and recipients. One could say that, at present, a healthy anarchy reigns.

The sheer volume of material available is surprising and potentially overwhelming to the newcomer. And appropriately enough these communication links are called 'super-highways'. Another form of communication link would use a CD ROM (a compact disk on which can be stored huge quantities of information at very high density – ROM stands for 'read only memory' which means that you cannot change it, you can only read it). This combined with the use of a broad band fibre optics[5] network is already being established in a piece-meal way for the transfer of huge quantities of information: films, videos, books and so on. One discussion at present is whether it will be PC or TV technology that will be used to display it. Either way, it looks as though trips to the video shop, and even maybe the library, will soon be a thing of the past.

One important question is, do these super-highways open up new opportunities for houseworkers? Does computer-mediated communication open up new opportunities for women – to communicate, to work and even to develop their ideas? The answer must be a guarded one. They will be swamped by the volume of information and they may not know of, or be able to afford, software to filter out what they want. Newsgroups and e-mail lists are useful, though experience shows that, given half a chance, some men will try to dominate them. Indeed 9 out 10 recognisable names given by 20 million Internet users are male (*The Guardian Weekend* 28 May 1994, p67). Women have certainly been on the receiving end of pornographic messages and suffered other unpleasant harassment. Dale Spender (1995) cites some particularly disturbing incidents.

Leaving aside the potential for harassment, how useful is e-mail as a form of personal communication? If you can be sure that the people to whom you wish to send a message regularly read their electronic mail, it is an efficient means of communication. To make telephone contact the person who is being called has to be available and free to talk. With electronic mail the recipient does not have to be available at the same time as the message is being sent; moreover, it allows the recipient to read the message when he or she chooses and allows time for considering a reply.

The way in which people tend to 'talk' with others on electronic mail is subtly

---

[5] Broad band fibre optics are cables that carry a number of signals simultaneously and, moreover, these signals can be sent at different frequencies so that some can be transmitted much faster than others. These light signals are carried down a glass tube much thinner than the traditional co-axial cable.

different from other forms of communication. Long and/or formal messages have the same style and form as they have on paper. Short requests and small pieces of information can be quite succinct when compared with a telephone call and this brevity does not seem to damage relationships. Some argue though, that the absence of accompanying features such as voice inflection and body language can on occasions produce ambiguity which can be misunderstood.

What I envisage is not just a network inside the household, but connections between households and between households and workplaces (I am not yet talking about teleworking). Messages to and from providers of all types of service – doctor, plumber, electrician and so on – could usefully be transferred to this medium. Lists of local service providers could be made available from which one could choose those about which one wanted more in-depth information. This is along the lines of PRESTEL which, as we have seen, has not been widely used. But the facility as I envisage it will be locally oriented. Messages between houseworkers about their work and social matters could broaden the horizons of those confined to work in the home.

So far I have been talking about computers linking home to the outside world in an interactive way where computer users 'talk' to one another both sending messages and receiving replies. There is, however, one very important facility one can access via the Internet which is not interactive in this way, namely the World-Wide Web or WWW. It is currently the most advanced information system deployed on the Internet. It includes a vast amount of data on an unrestricted range of topics.

The Web is so-called because information is structured in such a way that a reader can access it by following links in all directions through this mass of data. For example you can display a map of England and if you specify the location showing the name of my University (using an electronic pointer if you've got one) you will get an introductory page about the University. Similarly you can get a map of the University and 'point to' a department for information on its courses and research activities.

Use of the World-Wide Web is not interactive; you cannot type in messages in the way you do when you use e-mail. To add to or change the data you have to write your own pages and use special software to link them into the Web.

### Teleworking

Paradoxically, some forms of increased communications are restrictive. We have already seen that this is a disadvantage of teleshopping and telebanking. Teleworking is another case in point. Teleworking is doing paid work at home for an employer to whom you are linked by telecommunications and usually involves the electronic processing of information. Alternatively teleworkers are self-employed people working from home. Many of these, but by no means all, are women who work at home in order to dovetail their paid work with the work of bringing up children. British Telecom has produced a set of comprehensive reports (BT 1992) on this topic covering, as well as the impact on the environment and advantages for those with disabilities, the impact of teleworking on family life. Their report, *Clerical Teleworking – How it Affects Family Life*, suggests that flexibility between employer and employee is advantageous to both sides. It suggests encouraging women, when they wish to, to adjust their work patterns around their family life – although it would be regrettable if this meant women having to work in the small hours when the family is asleep. They address the problems of isolation, recognising that some people may even prefer to work alone but, on the other hand, suggesting that for others regular visits to the more usual place of work are important; and they note the advantages of electronic mail for maintaining communication among workers. There is no overwhelming tendency in the British Telecom reports to refer only to women – indeed at least one of the case studies quoted was a man – but nonetheless the report is primarily about employment arrangements for women.

A report of a further study of self-employed home-workers (Haddon and Silverstone 1994) suggests that the picture is not that rosy. The authors report how not going into an office means loss of self-esteem, social contacts, secretarial support and sick and holiday pay to these homeworkers. Family and friends tend not to regard such jobs as 'proper' jobs and feel free to ring for a chat and will not be deterred; children feel free to burst in with interruptions. Disruption to household arrangements is also reported, with partners having to wait to go to bed because the bedroom is used for work until late into the night.

Obviously more information is needed before one can draw reliable conclusions about the likely long-term benefits and disbenefits of teleworking for women, especially given the huge variation in personalities and circumstances. But if teleworking became widespread and a great number of women had to rely on this remote form of contact[6] (even if it did have video) the likelihood seems only too great that many women will be left

> ... living in something like a space-shuttle grounded on the earth – a private, home/work capsule – viewing the world through a rose-colored video screen (Zimmerman and Horwitz 1983, p121).

## Computers at Home – White Goods or Brown Goods?

I would argue that, at present, computers sold in the high street are sold as brown goods. But what would happen if computers were used for domestic homework at least in the very few ways I have sketched, and if this work were still perceived as women's work? Would they then become white goods? Or would we then have two types of computers? One sort might have an exterior, monitor, mouse and keyboard designed with women and their work in mind, and the other would be for men, designed to please their aesthetic tastes and to cater for their hobbies and pastimes.

It would be nice to think that the very introduction of computers into the home in ways that we have not yet imagined would have the much wider effect of blurring this genderising of household technology.

---

[6]Significantly, computer people sometimes talk of handshakes; rather than suggesting social interaction it turns out that the only things talking to one another are machines!

## Technology that Ought to be There

Frances GABe (1983) spent 27 years inventing a self-cleaning house to save herself the perpetual drudgery of housework. Her principle is not to clean a dirty house but to keep a clean house clean. Clothes, linen are all cleaned *in situ* and, for example, there are Dishwasher Cupboards (the upper case letters are hers) where she keeps and cleans her single set of crockery. A General Room Washing Apparatus cleans her rooms with a warm mist under controlled pressure. Her equipment incorporating the latest sophisticated computer control would surely save houseworkers time. And why, if we have the Strategic Defence Initiative, all those engaging ideas mooted in *The Electronic Frontier* and BT's Home of the Future, can't we have technology like Frances GABe's. Her inventions really would save time and, along with other sociological changes, release women to pursue their own lives.

Anne-Jorunn Berg confirms this view of slow progress on the home front. She describes some recent projects for the design of the 'supposed technological home of the future' or 'smart' house (Berg 1994). She even relates how one of the projects had plans, but emphatically only plans, for a cleaning cupboard like those that Frances GABe pioneered some 30 years earlier. However, the whole spirit of GABe's project was quite different from those Berg studied. The designers in the projects Berg describes were men, designing houses for other men who would share their fascination with technological gadgetry, people in their own image and not housewives. Indeed these men were surprised to be asked questions on housework issues.

Frances GABe had to overcome incredulity from a local official, architects and builders over aspects of her self-cleaning house. If women are not to end up as perpetual Cinderellas, there has to be a change of attitude. They have to learn to take control of technology in general and computing in particular, including the hardware and the software and the way it is used, in order to ensure that it is they who dictate what is done, how it's done and where it's done.

Incidentally, I'm not convinced that household robots are the long-term answer. The more lasting solutions, when they come, will be more radical and less manly than that.

# Part III

# Women, Computing and Employment – What It's Like Now

# 4

# How Men Hog the Stage . . .

*Women have shown fitness for the highest social functions, exactly in proportion as they have been admitted to them.* Harriet Taylor Mill 1851 (Mill 1970a, p102)

## 4.1   Where are All the Women?

Throughout history women have been deprived of the life-chances men have enjoyed in virtually all spheres, to the great disadvantage of women and the equally great disadvantage of the societies in which they lived. For all its modernity, the contemporary sphere of computing is proving no exception to this rule. It may be new, but it has been introduced into a world of old values by people with old values, including those which relegate women to second place.

It may seem odd to ask where all the women are. Go into any open plan office where computers are being used and you may well see a fair representation of women. But probe a little more and you will discover that they are doing low status jobs for low pay and many of them will be using their computers merely for clerical work: data-entry and word-processing. How many of the men you see will be using their machines for such clerical jobs – and all day long? On the other hand, offices outside the open area are mostly filled with men who are evidently in higher status managerial roles.

## 4.2   Jobs for the Girls?

There was a time in the early years of computing when women made up many of the few programmers then at work. As I shall note again in Chapter 5, Women's Royal Naval Service personnel worked on deciphering Enigma signals during World War II. In the 1940s in the United States a group of women known as the 'ENIAC girls' programmed an early computer called the ENIAC. There is also anecdotal evidence that in the 1960s and '70s the proportion of women programmers was really quite high (Gunter 1994). As I go on to say in Chapter 5, this was originally based on the mistaken view that programming is a merely clerical job. Once it was realised that programming required a higher level skill than this, men have been ensuring their own domination in this type of job.

The result of this male encroachment is that, according to one survey, in 1991 fewer than two in ten (18%) higher status jobs in computing were held by women. Contrast this with seven out of ten lower status jobs held by women. By higher status jobs I mean systems and data processing managers, analysts and programmers; by lower status I mean data entry clerks and other clerical workers (LFS 1991).

Another sample, also from 1991 (WIT 1992), confirms this general level of women in the higher status jobs. The figures in Table 4.1 show the percentages of women holding six different types of these jobs. The final row shows the percentage of women in all of these categories taken together (as distinct from taking the average of the percentages given in the table); the figure is 21%, broadly confirming the 18% of the first survey. The percentage of women in the first two, managerial, categories taken together is 12%.

| Job Title | Percentage of Females |
|---|---|
| Data Processing Manager | 3 |
| Project Manager | 14 |
| Systems Analyst | 29 |
| Analyst Programmer | 25 |
| Programmer I | 23 |
| Systems Programmer | 13 |
| Total | 21 |

**Table 4.1:** *Women Employed in Computing (Software) 1991*

There is another category which, as we shall see later, while not of high status is nonetheless important and this is the category of computer technicians and engineers. For these the proportion of women is less than one in ten (WIT 1992).

This is a really extraordinary situation made all the more extraordinary by the fact that women by and large accept their subordinate position and hardly question it. I describe the situation as extraordinary and yet in one sense it is not at all extraordinary – it is the norm outside the world of computing as well as inside it. That it is already the norm does of course help men to establish and retain a dominant position in a new sphere like computing.

As I explained in Chapter 1, I was seconded from my usual place of work in higher education to spend twelve months working in a District Health Authority (DHA). Arriving as I did new to the scene, sensitive to the behaviour of women and men, I was able to observe what happened with a fresh eye. As a relative outsider

I was able to stand back a bit from the situation and, at the same time, be heavily involved in the work of the department – as a kind of participant observer.

Once again the extraordinary thing was not just the subordination of women, but the way in which they did not challenge this situation; indeed they went further and tended to disapprove of anyone who did challenge it. One thing that struck me was the way in which communication between men and women reflected all the views and *mores* to be found generally in society and how this contributed strongly to the acquiescence of women. Modes of communication are so much part of the texture and fabric of everyday experience in the workplace, it is difficult to stand back from them and see what effects they have. So I shall shortly spend some time examining this subject.

But before doing so, it would help if I gave a brief description of the staff and structure of the DHA department where I worked and of the working environment. Of course workplaces are not all the same; there are considerable differences. Some are better than the one I am about to describe, some are worse. I particularly want to describe a workplace I experienced which was not at either of these extremes and which is typical of many.

## 4.3   Communication in the Workplace

### The Workplace

The department, which produced computer systems, consisted, at a point six months in to the secondment, of a male head of department, 9 women and 16 men, excluding secretarial staff. There was some hierarchical structure beneath the head of department – but not much. Most of the staff were fairly recent employees and, on the whole, young. Of those directly concerned with software production and hardware maintenance, 7 were women and 14 were men, so one third of these staff were women. Three of these men were responsible for hardware, purchasing and installing new equipment; these I refer to as technical staff and there was a mini hierarchical structure here, with one of these three in charge.

The room in which I worked was a large, old computer room (designed originally to house 1960s mainframes) which by then contained programmers and some of the machines. It was, in effect, a large open plan office with minimal partitioning.

### Topics of Conversation – Computing and Non-computing

In the programming room the men talked loudly about plans for the department (who was to use what machine, how machines were to be configured and so on – discussions in which women were rarely involved as equals). By doing this, they not only went a long way towards establishing exactly how things would be organised, but also achieved amongst themselves a sense of domination over the women.

Such discussion about computing matters – and this is particularly true of hardware – bonds men together, possibly to form alliances against the 'threat' posed by women. (The apparent alternative explanation that they just don't notice the women only makes the same point in a different way.) Given that technology is part of the male identity (and I shall have more to say about this later), to talk about it in front of women and, at one and the same time, to exclude women from those conversations, is to form and strengthen bonds between men. Male bonding and the exclusion of women are part and parcel of one another, two sides of the same coin.

It was not only by talking about computing matters that the men maintained their dominant position. They also used selected non-computing matters that were recognised as appropriate for men and not for women (cars, car-insurance, social drinking, football, aircraft, cricket, etc.). When women participated in discussions of these things they only rarely did so with deep-seated interest. If that interest was well-founded, then they might be accepted as 'one of the boys', but even then they were accepted only as supplicants. This was a type of acceptance that did not give them access to the power making functions. Rather it ensured that, although they may have been quite close to these functions, they were under control and could be kept from the central power-base. Some women refused to earn their credentials by showing interest in male topics. These women were more of a threat to the *status quo* than those who did; they demonstrated that they were not under the same kind of control.

It was not only by means of the choice of topic that the men asserted their dominance, they also talked loudly and thus publicly – except, that is, when there was an obvious benefit to be had from talking quietly. By doing so they were implicitly claiming the right to hold forth on these matters and that it was the women's duty to listen and accept their pronouncements. So volume, and tone of voice, in this open plan setting were factors which, along with the selection of topics, helped significantly to keep women in their place.

When women stated their objections to these conversational *mores* it was they who were at fault. Of one woman, who found the environment difficult to work in, it was said that she 'must be more flexible' if she wanted her contract renewed. In other words, if she was not at least prepared to live with the noise and male dominance she would not be allowed to stay. Female topics of conversation were carried on between women *sotto voce* and away from the centre of power. You would rarely hear women talking about non-computing matters such as housework, pregnancy or child care, or even about computing matters, in such loud volumes across the programming room. These so-called 'female' topics were a source of barely concealed amusement to the dominant men – as we shall see later, ridicule is, of course, an important tool in any power game.

Women who stand back from, or even walk away from, what I call 'men's power conversations' are identifying themselves as women who are not primarily interested in pleasing men. Since the conversations held in these work contexts mirror those held in purely social contexts, those who did not want to join in deprived themselves of much of the social life of the department. This involved activities such as going to lunch together, social conversations within the workplace, the occasional visit to the pub and 'Skirmish', a commando-type war game which was played in local woods at the weekends. The social life is important because it is another context in which this power game is continued.

## Male Perception of Women in the Workplace

If you listen carefully to the tone in which men talk about women and the words that they use to describe women in their absence, you will find that some men (not all) use quite a different tone from the one they use to talk about men. If they have something derisive or derogatory to say about a woman, they often say 'There's this woman in Department X who . . .' with the unnecessary and irrelevant emphasis on the gender of the subject. If, on the other hand, they are to be derisive about a man, his gender will not be mentioned. To introduce gender when deriding a woman appears to reinforce the argument. Some in the DHA computing department used the word 'bitching' to describe the complaints of those outside the department about some aspect of their system. Though not everybody used this expression themselves, the use of it by some was accepted. This term was not used simply to refer to women but to men and women alike. In this instance, when people were to be derided it was done using words that implied a peculiarly female nastiness (whatever that may be).

## Gender-biased Language

I should not end this section without mentioning the widely recognised effects of the use of gender-biased language, e.g. using 'he' when it should be 'he or she'. This is regularly done when the jobs are of high status – the converse often happens when lower status jobs are being referred to, for example, nurses and cleaners were always referred to as 'she', as if no males were to be found in these 'inferior' positions. As we shall see, this sort of language is used in the classroom as well as the workplace. In the classroom those who regularly use 'he' where they should use 'he or she' can be construed as not only referring to males and describing a male-oriented world, but also as addressing primarily the men amongst the listeners.

The use of gender-biased language has often been questioned and its effect on women examined (e.g. Dale Spender (1990) and Deborah Cameron (1985)). I shall discuss this question at greater length in Chapter 7. How far a change in language will improve women's perception of the profession and the environment is a complex issue; not all changes in language produce changes of attitude. But it is enough to say for the moment that even if a change in language will not bring a change of attitude, we will not get a shift of attitude without a change in language.

## 4.4   The Role of Computer Hardware

Traditionally, technicians' posts in these computing departments are held almost entirely by men. Certainly this has been my personal experience and data collected by Computer Economics for October 1991 suggest that nationally around only 8%

of this staff are female ((WIT 1992) and personal communication with Computer Economics). This segregation is yet another contribution to the power structure. In the DHA computing department hardware was purchased as ready-made components. The skill that technicians required lay in 'bolting' these components together. While managers may say women are encouraged to get involved, this is misleading. Women are deterred at the outset by the extra scrutiny which they know full well their work will be given, and the subliminal mirth at the very presence of women amongst the men who have control of the hardware – mirth which most women are not prepared to risk. As Judy Wajcman observes, 'Women's identity is not enhanced by their use of machines' (Wajcman 1991, p89). In practice, in this environment the distinction between hardware and software is blurred. These men had very much the same type of skills as the programmers, skills which women have as well; an important part of their job was, for example, installing software. And insofar as the skills involved were different (using soldering irons, screwdrivers, etc. and carrying equipment round) there was absolutely no reason why women could not do it. Yet it is doubtful if these technicians, or anyone else in the department, would have accepted a woman in that team on an equal footing with the men.

This seems to be a particular instance of a general phenomenon. How often do you see a woman engineer repair your washing machine or the departmental photocopier?

To relinquish this work to women would mean the invasion of an important stronghold of gender stereotyping – important not for the sheer number of technicians' jobs involved nor for their status (they do not enjoy a particularly high status) but more generally in a symbolic way. If these jobs were 'lost' to women, all men would suffer because masculine self-image would be blurred by this loss.

A further point worth making on this question of access to hardware is that male programmers who have acquired some hardware skills often regard themselves as superior computing practitioners because they believe that the benefits of these hardware skills spill over into other types of computer work. I suspect that if, *per impossibile*, women occupied a high proportion of these technicians' jobs or simply acquired some of their skills, then this supposed advantage and aura would disappear.

## 4.5   Role Models

It is interesting to note, in passing, how this male dominance of the computing scene subverts a factor generally supposed to be helpful to women, namely role models. For years it has been argued that if only girls and young women could see their elders succeed, then they would want to emulate them. Consequently, senior women are regularly asked to speak at conferences and workshops and to talk about their experiences in order to encourage girls to enter the profession. In spite of this, as we have already seen, girls still don't seem to be coming forward.

I would suggest that female role models are often counter-productive. Many potential women recruits to the professions are deterred by these successful women.

The main reason for this is not hard to find. Open modern women's magazines and amongst the articles on 'Work' you will find advice which, on the face of it, is positive about gaining confidence, dealing with verbal abuse and socialising. It advises women to 'Stop the Stereotype' and to avoid a situation where

> They attack, you defend; they shout, you shout back; they become aggressive, you become the little woman (New Woman 1993*b*, p160).

On the 'if you can't beat them, join them' principle, these magazine articles present a list entitled 'Tactics that Work' in which it is suggested to the reader that 'If you work mostly with men, take an interest in the subjects that appeal to them!' (New Woman 1993*a*, p157) So, if a woman wants to get on, she must not fight the system, she must act compliantly and should be able to talk knowledgeably about football, cricket and cars.

But this is negative advice advocating a sycophantic participation in the practices of male dominance. It reinforces women's belief that their traditional role is an inferior one, rather than asking them to re-evaluate that role. Thus role models provide support for this male dominance at the same time as they appear to be counter examples to it. One moderately successful, acquiescent woman in a computing department provides all that is needed for those in authority to say, 'We do promote women. Look at Ms X.'

But what do girls see when presented with Ms X? They see, in reality, only a very few Ms Xs, most of them have not got very far and many need to have worked extremely hard to get even that little distance. Above all, girls see them compromising their identity as women.[1] And, interestingly, many successful women

---

[1] In another context, Grace Hopper (1906–92), who helped to pioneer the introduction of the programming

do not seem to be very keen to see other women follow them. How much did the first British woman Prime Minister, Margaret Thatcher[2], do to help or encourage other women to succeed? This whole scene, as far as role models are concerned, discourages emulation. There are certainly a few who are not discouraged and are tolerant of this suppression of individual identity – indeed there will be a few whose individual identity chimes in well with football, cricket and cars. But for most women and, one suspects, many men, these topics do not appeal. And in the vast majority of cases involvement in these conversations involves a distortion of personality.

For female role models to be really what they appear to be, a sign of growing equality of opportunity, there would have to be a corresponding recognition by men that if there were more women at the top, some men would be bound to be displaced 'downwards'. At present all that young men see is their male superiors working hard to maintain their dominant position. (As we shall see in the next section, one of the main things they learn is how to inculcate guilt in feminist women and to ridicule their position.) The occasional concession by men to female emancipation is for a few men to disappear at odd times, professedly to participate more fully in domestic work at home. Men are just beginning to participate in 'domestic' work that needs doing in the workplace: making coffee (for themselves), photocopying (for themselves), arranging appointments (for themselves) and meals (which they themselves will eat). The present power structure ensures that, by and large, these jobs are still carried out by women; there are no initiatives that I know of to recruit more male secretaries.

## 4.6  'They Burn their Bras, Don't They?' Guilt and Ridicule – The Ultimate Weapons

If we start with the premise that there is a consensus that feminist progress has to be curtailed and if possible stopped, then it is revealing to try and answer the question: What is the best and most efficient way to achieve this end?

In spite of the fact that they are seldom recognised as such, guilt and ridicule are extremely powerful weapons in the struggle between men and women in the computing arena as elsewhere.

It is generally counter-productive to impose 'external' punishment on those who step out of line by, for example, insisting on putting a woman's point of view or objecting to sexual harassment. Such punishment tends to highlight the disadvantaged position of women and to make something of a martyr of those who protest.

What is needed is something far more subtle. If men, consciously or unconsciously, can induce guilt in potential offenders and the punishment is thus

---

language COBOL and rose to high rank in the US Navy, was always presented in the computing press in a naval uniform – though of course she was a non-combatant.
    [2] Margaret Thatcher was Conservative Prime Minister from 1979 to 1990

internalised, it becomes self-generating. Once that is done, there is no need for those who seek to control to do anything except occasionally remind offenders that they are doing harm to what the men fondly regard as the greatest number – themselves and their colleagues. In this way the 'guilty' police themselves, their consciences do the men's work for them and men have no need to appear as oppressors.[3] The motivation is stifled at birth.

One way of triggering guilt is to respond to feminist arguments with 'You are doing your cause no good. You are bringing it into disrepute and letting other women down as is shown by the fact that they don't all agree with you.' The 'logic' behind this position seems to be that there is a momentum towards equality which the men concerned approve of and, indeed, contribute to. But if you misguidedly insist on trying to speed up that momentum with these 'extremist' views, there will be no choice but to slow the momentum down. In this way you are inhibiting the progress of all women and indeed working against the general public good. Guilt and shame on you!

To raise the subject of women's position at all except in gatherings convened explicitly for the purpose is to cause embarrassment – to induce in the speaker extreme guilt that she or he has committed a social solecism and has 'gone beyond the bounds of propriety'. Discussion of sexual discrimination is taboo – as taboo as the subject of sexual intercourse.

One of the oldest and most effective ways of undermining an opponent's

---

[3] cf 'Whose Mum didn't use Persil?'

position is to bring it into ridicule by caricaturing it. Thus one way of brushing aside all feminists' rational arguments is to come out with statements like 'They burn their bras, don't they?' or 'She's the sort of person who insists we should say 'Personchester' instead of 'Manchester' ' or 'They kick men's shins you know' or 'She's strident'.

Other subtle forms abound. We have already seen how there is subliminal mirth when women embark on technicians' work and they try to organise technical equipment. Women's activities within the educational environment, like workshops for schoolgirls to experience computing, still tend to cause amusement in some computing departments. Defending women colleagues who have been generally deemed 'neurotic' will prompt ridicule. We have already seen in Chapter 3 that the domestic level is the nadir for computing and how suggesting domestic applications for computers prompted laughter. It is for just the same sort of reason that Cynthia Cockburn told how she seldom failed to bring a smile to people's faces whenever she mentioned that she was making a study of the social relations surrounding the microwave oven.[4]

Guilt and ridicule each has its own independent effect; guilt induces a sense of unworthiness, ridicule a sense of humiliation. Both are designed to make a feminist feel isolated and outcast and want to get back into the fold. There is no reason to believe that guilt and ridicule are any less effective in computing than elsewhere.

---

[4] Opening remarks to Women into Computing Conference 1992.

# 5

# ... And Keep Centre Stage: Purism, Elitism & Sexism

*Think what it is to be a boy, to grow up to manhood in the belief that without any merit or exertion of his own, though he may be the most frivolous and empty or the most ignorant and stolid of mankind, by the mere fact of having been born a male he is by right the superior of all and every one of an entire half of the human race: including probably some whose real superiority to himself he has daily or hourly occasion to feel . . .* John Stuart Mill 1869 (Mill 1984, p324)

In identifying some of the mechanisms that contribute to male domination we have, so far, examined a few of the behavioural patterns of groups of individuals and aspects of communication between them. In this chapter we look at the differences among types of work and the way in which men make use of these differences to support their position. We look first at the 'pure' centre of computing which is largely inhabited by and is certainly controlled by men. Not only is this centre controlled by men, it is the controlling point for computing. As we move away from this central point where machines are untainted by human foibles, we move to less 'pure'– and less prestigious – arenas where women (and men) work.

## 5.1   The Pure and the Messy

There is a kind of 'pure', abstract computing work which is unadulterated and prestigious and in which men get intensely involved. To move away from this world of pure computing to the real world in which the end-user works, is to move to work that is no longer pure because it is tainted by the demands and exigencies of the more ordinary, work-a-day world. Men see it as their right and prerogative to work in this rarefied world of what might facetiously be termed 'virtual reality' and indeed tend to get more intensively involved in it than do women.

## Pure, Abstract Computing

First, what do I mean by this world of 'pure', 'rarefied', 'virtual reality' computing? Sherry Turkle (1984*a*) (Turkle and Papert 1990) identifies the different approaches of various categories of people to computing. She talks of the holding power that computers have for many of these people: hackers, video game addicts and so on. This mesmeric effect is common amongst many who work in the industry. Paul Edwards suggests that:

> What gives the computer this power . . . is the simulated world entirely within the machine itself, that does not depend on instrumental effectiveness. That is, where most tools produce effects on a wider world of which they are only a part, the computer contains its own worlds in miniature. Artificial intelligence researchers have called the simulated world within the computer 'microworlds' (Edwards 1990, p109).

Paul Edwards points to the striking parallel between the military culture and the microworld of computing – a parallel that is not so surprising once one realizes the great influence of military needs in the second world war and subsequently on the development of computing. He points to their shared gamelike structure. Both, particularly in the era of possible total annihilation, are played in an abstract mode with the object of maintaining 'a winning *scenario*' instead of actually fighting. However, the important point for present purposes is the 'cultural fit, between the cognitive hard mastery of computer science research and the strategic situation of contemporary militarism'. Also contributing to the 'gamelike structure of these microworlds' are their common characteristics: their 'hierarchies, strict laws of conduct, chains of command, orders, uniforms, and precise jargon' (Edwards 1990, p114).

The parallels between computer games and modern nuclear warfare are striking: the tidiness and aseptic nature of the electronic battlefield as compared with the real one, the shared gamelike structure of *Space Invaders* and the version of engagements in the Gulf War that appear on military screens. It is possible to operate within these gamelike microworlds without what goes off in the real world having anything like its full impact.

My own observations bear out what others have said, that it is largely men who get involved in these microworlds (Turkle 1984*a*, Hacker 1981). There are increasing fears that electronic games, which are largely used by males 'may not be merely non-educational but anti-educational in that they discourage social interaction' (EIU 1993). If boys and men are allowed to devote themselves to these non-social activities and, eventually, obtain superior rewards for doing so, then women are left to deal with the work that requires interactive social skills which are valued less highly.

Thus – and feminists argue similarly in other contexts – it is usually women who have to deal with reality, which is 'messy'. The messy and untidy tasks, such as bringing up children who have unpredictable needs, are relegated to the domestic sphere. These jobs are left to the women, just as organising a man's semi-private life is often left to his less highly paid female secretary. So too in the computing world, messy jobs are left for the women to do.

## The 'Messy' and Untidy

Let me give an example of what I mean by a 'messy' job. The correct identification of individuals within a computer system is critical in the Health Service as it is in many other businesses: building societies, public services, banks and so on. Not getting this right is costly, yet when teaching, although we know the problems exist, we ignore them. Take, for example, a job that required merging two databases by matching patient records in each. In both they were identified by the same demographic data: last name, first name and date of birth. But, in view of the sensitivity of the data (one database was a death register) we had to check each potential match visually. Out of approximately four thousand records in one database, only 1500 were obvious matches, the rest had minor and major differences. Where there were differences, possible matches had to be located and compared. Decisions as to which demographic items could be used for these possible matches, what language the programs should be written in, estimates of how long the programming would take and how long the programs would take to run – all required some skill. There are always numerous other important jobs like this to be done.

Endemic though this type of problem is, no one seems to be trained to deal with it. I certainly have never taught students how to tackle this type of problem. At the moment teachers and assessors of students' work actually reward an insular attitude. We minimise the need to understand and cope with the connections that the computer has with the outside world. 'It's messy, it's untidy' – how often can those words be heard in computer science departments, implying that 'We don't want it here'. Training to deal with the messy tasks is not usually given a place in our curricula and it will require major effort to get it introduced. Indeed, counter arguments will be urged such as 'We must teach them the fundamentals first', 'Students cannot possibly tackle these problems until they learn the basic skills.' These arguments are undoubtedly valid, but the 'untidy' is excluded at a cost. When these students graduate and move to the workplace, those who teach themselves to bring something useful out of the mess are of course 'very much appreciated' but largely unrewarded. Those who stay in the microworld are rewarded with kudos and promotion.

As I have already said, it is men who get involved in the microworlds and women who are left the task of relating them to reality. There seemed to be a tendency, in the Health Authority workplace at least, to leave not only the messy tasks to women but also the tedious ones. (Some messy jobs aren't tedious and some tedious jobs aren't messy.) Writing report programs to summarise various aspects of a database, though not messy, was a less glamorous and often tedious job left largely to women staff. 'That's all she's fit for' was said of a woman who, it was suggested, could write some of these. Women were efficient and careful at these apparently pedestrian tasks. And, if you left women to do it, it most probably was done more efficiently than if you left it to the men who could get away with either not doing it, or doing it badly, confident in the knowledge that someone else (usually a woman) would be persuaded to complete it. (We all know the (deliberately) poor quality of work some men produce when asked, for example, to do the ironing.)

So sexism, while preventing women's access to highly valued jobs, can at the same time be efficient – in the short run, that is. But in the long run, this allocation of labour along gender lines ignores the fact that some women are better than some men at the pure computing. Or, to put it another way, some men are over-stretching themselves doing the pure computing when some women could do it better.

## Formal Methods and 'Hacking'

What I have just described is the current division of labour between the pure and the messy. It is interesting to speculate just how this division will proceed in the future, particularly with the greater use of 'formal methods' to which this distinction between the pure and the messy also applies.

Formal methods is a branch of computer science and part of the broader subject of 'software engineering'; the term refers to the use of mathematical techniques for software development. They are used to verify that software is correct before it is written in a programming language or, to use the jargon, 'coded'. There are formal languages with clearly defined rules of syntax which can be used for the specification and verification of software (two of these are the Vienna Development Method, or VDM, and Z) but their notations, quite deliberately, do not bear any direct resemblance to any programming language.

Formal methods are relatively new. Early academic developments occurred in the 1970s and their advancement is encouraged by the idea that constructing a theoretical model prior to implementation or programming permits checking out that model and seeing that it works. Thus formal methods provide the means to prove that the planned software precisely meets the original specification.

The distinction between the pure and the messy in the case of formal methods is between those who do the pure abstract thinking and those who do the program coding or the 'hackers'. Nowadays the word 'hacker' has a range of meanings. It means those who illegally read other people's files and corrupt or misuse software (sometimes just for the hell of it). At the good end of the hacking spectrum is the hacker who just enjoys programming and developing more and more sophisticated programming tricks – 'a person who pursues innovations of stylistic and technical brilliance, not solely for constructive goals, but with some wild pleasure in the mere involvement'. Some way towards the middle, away from the malicious end, there is also the 'bad hacker' who 'lunges around in a fairly uncontrolled fashion on the basis of try and see – a bodger' (Harding 1993, p26 & p27). We are concerned here with the latter two types – hackers who are non-malicious.

So we have on the one hand the pure, disciplined abstract thinkers mindful of, but not involved in, actually making the thing work, the software engineers expert at formal methods. On the other hand we have the immature, undisciplined hackers or programmers getting their hands 'dirty' with program code.

There is, however, a view that with dramatically more powerful hardware and similarly sharp decreases in the cost of memory there will be, by the end of this century, relatively little need for conventional programming skills. This trend will be accentuated by the increased use of formal methods. The improvement in hardware will lead to a concomitant improvement in the software. These improvements will mean, at any rate for a narrow range of tasks, that a system can be specified in one of these formal languages. Programs known as *automatic code generators* will translate these specifications in the formal language into program code which the computer can run without further human intervention.

There are other examples where this kind of procedure could prevail; one is in the use of Computer Aided Software Engineering or CASE tools. These have been employed for many years now. Their use can, very broadly speaking, be compared with that of formal methods. Using them alone does not, at present, produce a complete system although those who market them will no doubt claim that they do. They allow a designer to design a system using various types of diagram, charts and pseudo-code (this is code written in an English-like language, but very formal, and bearing more resemblance to a programming language than to English). However, these tools do not allow for the mathematical rigour of formal languages like VDM.

The vision is that these 'higher level' techniques and tools will develop to such an extent that programmers will no longer be needed. The skills that systems designers and those who are at present called programmers will have will be partly in using these and partly in integrating the use of existing packages. To some extent, this is already happening (Peltu 1994).

But as Ed Yourdon suggests, 'People will still be programming in assembler and C for a long time.' (Yourdon 1993, p272) (Assembler is a type of primitive programming language widely used in the early days because there were no other more sophisticated languages available. C is, now, a widely used language whose cryptic syntax can cause some *angst* to newcomers.) Yourdon's prediction is quite likely to come true. To say the least, there is a huge amount of software around that will not be quickly replaced if past experience is anything to go by, and which will still need maintenance by programmers. And certainly somebody has to write these automatic code generators in the first instance – and that requires programming skills.

The questions for our present purposes are 'What will be the hierarchy amongst these tasks?' 'How will they be viewed by managers?' 'Will some have a higher status and command better pay than others?' 'Will some be for men and some for women?' 'Insofar as ordinary programming is still practised by the year 2000, will it be a low status job mainly done by women?'

I am not suggesting that these two activities, software engineering and programming, are presently job-gendered and that only men do the abstract thinking and women the programming. There are some female software engineers and certainly there are many men hacking away at their keyboards. But there is debate about the relative benefits of the two modes of software production and, moreover, the job-gendering for these tasks is still in a state of flux and under negotiation – although this is not generally realised. What I am suggesting is that the clean and tidy formal methods approach with its 'sound mathematical basis' will come out on top and will be appropriated by men. The hackers will be relegated to the 'shop floor of IT' and whether those who do these jobs will be men – mechanics – or whether they will be women – typists – I don't yet know.

## 5.2   Sexist Skill Evaluation

I use the term *sexist skill evaluation* to refer to the widespread phenomenon of high evaluation of skills that are appropriated by men where men predominate in the execution of that skill, and the correspondingly low evaluation of jobs that require skills acquired by and expected of women. Men and women may do the same jobs, but when women do them, they are less highly regarded than when men do them. And there is an equivalent sexist *role* evaluation.[1] Along with these different levels of evaluation go corresponding levels of job valuation – or, to put it more prosaically, higher rates of pay for men's jobs and lower rates of pay for women's.

The most obvious example is the evaluation of domestic work. As everyone knows, not only does this type of work receive a low evaluation but, when performed by the traditional housewife, no pay at all – it is not generally considered to be work. Domestic work, particularly cleaning, when performed outside the home receives low financial rewards and conditions of employment for domestic workers are generally poor.

Domestic work is a distinct example of job segregation which makes comparative job evaluation extremely difficult: so long as women are doing one type of job and men another, differential rates of pay are easy to defend. There are other examples besides domestic work. Cynthia Cockburn describes how lay-making (the laying out of patterns to make optimum use of cloth) in pattern rooms of clothing manufacturers was a skilled job done largely by men before the introduction of Computer Aided Design (CAD) systems. As the task became automated, or semi-automated, it was apparently gradually handed over to women and considered less skilled (Cockburn 1985, Chapter 2). Skill was still needed when doing the job in a semi-automated or interactive mode, for example when making human interventions in the computerised lay-making procedure to improve the use of materials, but these skills are now ignored. Lay-making is considered the least skilled job in the pattern room.

This example is unlike the housework example in that the job has been done both by men and by women. When men did it, it was deemed highly skilled but, as techniques for executing the work changed, it was gradually feminised and simultaneously became 'deskilled'. Computerisation of skills, feminisation and deskilling all occur together. Or, more accurately, feminisation and deskilling both occur together and computerisation usually shifts the job towards a 'downmarket'

---

[1] A good example of this was provided by Lisa Jardine in *The Guardian* 'When it was announced that I was leaving Cambridge to take up a professorship at the University of London, a senior colleague leant across the table at a meeting to congratulate me, "Good men aren't staying in the profession any more," he confided, "academic life doesn't have the status it used to have" ' (*The Guardian* 12 May 1993, p18).

position. Occasionally computerisation may shift a job 'upmarket' and cause it to appear more skilled, in which case the men gain or maintain a monopoly of it. These simultaneous developments make it extremely difficult to compare jobs before and after computerisation. But no matter what the relative skills required, the fact remains that when men did the job it was deemed skilled and now that women do it it has become 'unskilled'.

At this point it is worth looking briefly at the history of women's role in the computer industry.

Punched cards, which were widely used for the input of data and programs until the late 1970s, were prepared almost entirely by women because the keyboard skills required are similar to those of a typist. I still vividly remember in the 1970s, as the only woman programmer/advisor in a computer centre, being the only person asked to punch cards when the department was short of punch card operators, although my male colleagues were just as available as I was. Computer operators who operated (as in some organisations they still do) the physically relatively large computers, loading tapes and disks, and who work at the centre of computing activity, were, and still are in my experience, nearly all male and are nearly always managed by men. In a parallel way, during nearly 30 years of continuous employment in computing I have never seen a woman engineer called out to repair a computer.

The history of women's role in the software industry is less well-defined. As I noted earlier, women operated early computational devices; in Britain hundreds of women from the Women's Royal Naval Service were employed deciphering Enigma signals on COLOSSUS in 1943–4 (Lavington 1980). In the United States the 'ENIAC girls' were employed to program the ENIAC computer in the mid 1940s – largely because it was assumed that programming was a clerical job similar to using a mechanical calculator. Once the job had been redefined as intellectually demanding and creative, the women were gradually eased out (Kraft 1979). Subsequently, many women entered programming in '60s and early '70s who had a background in mathematics and other disciplines. In spite of these early influxes and the new prominence of computing in the 1980s, women are still less numerous in software jobs. As we saw in Chapter 4, in 1991 the percentage of women employed in computer software jobs was around 20%.

Men and women are now trained to do most types of software jobs, but as I have indicated with the DHA, men seem to be appropriating a subset of these – those that are more highly valued than the jobs that the women are doing.

## 5.3 From High Priests to 'Peasants and Blockheads'

Bearing in mind the phenomenon of sexist skill evaluation, I want now to consider the relation of the hardware to different types of jobs connected with computing.

Earlier I introduced the discussion of the messy and the tedious by describing how it is possible to live in a kind of computing microworld divorced from much of reality, how men are more prone to do this than women and how this leads them to value and appropriate those jobs that avoid the mess and untidiness of dealing with the real world. I identified this computing microworld as the centre of power: male power. As we move outwards from this centre, the power is diluted and at the same time more and more women become involved in computing activities.

In the workplace, the first step away from the centre is into the world of programmers, of whom only 21% are women (LFS 1991). We have also just seen how jobs are becoming segregated within this band, with women doing the messy undervalued jobs and men doing the pure and prestigious ones. The next band of people, as we move out from the centre, are the end-users; these are those who use the systems that the programmers 'build'. Here again there is a high level of gender segregation in the different types of activity that take place.

## Attitudes of Implementors towards End-Users

If there was elitism on the part of the pure computer men separating them from the women doing the messy and untidy work within the DHA computing department, this elitism characterised even more markedly the relationship between those who worked in the computing department and outsiders who were not members of the department but used the systems. Thus there was a series of bands with the pure at the centre, messy programming in the middle and end-users on the outside. As one progressed through these bands, power and prestige diminished and the proportion of women using the machines increased. (I am talking here of the power derived from the computing context.)

Let us first look at the different types of end-user in our hospital environment. The work of the DHA computing department was to provide systems (primarily database systems) to assist in patient administration in both clinical and administrative hospital departments. The end-users of the systems included:

1. Clerks who compile statistical data for return to various departments

2. Clerks who process contract data

3. Ward clerks

4. Nurses

5. Departmental secretaries

6. Medical laboratory technicians

7. Consultants

The first five categories were made up largely of women and the laboratory technicians who used these systems were also mainly women. The only category which, insofar as my dealings with it were concerned, was entirely male was the last – the consultants.

It was women who input almost all the data. (The only place I encountered men inputting data was in reception in Accident & Emergency.) The systems were commissioned by their managers, and written by men and women in ways already described, but it was women who operated them.

The computing systems required by consultants were for the recording of data for audit and administrative purposes. Hardware and software had not yet reached the stage of development where they could be used in the consulting room or clinic for suggesting diagnoses or drugs (as distinct from merely printing out the prescription). So these computer systems were used for recording historical events. Much of this could be recorded after the interview with the patient. Some could have been recorded while the patient was present, but little was. The consultants handed over the input to others. (Sometimes, on the other hand, computerisation of things like personal records has led men to do more of their own clerical work.)

It will be interesting to watch how the allocation of these tasks proceeds as alternative forms of input, such as speech, become more readily available. Speech input will clearly leave consultants free to use their hands. Will male consultants be prepared to speak into a machine rather than pressing keys on a keyboard? What status will this inputting process have when keyboards are no longer prevalent?

We have, therefore, outside the computing department, in place of the card punch operators of the '60s and '70s, female clerks typing data on keyboards and men commissioning new systems for the female operators to use.

The elitist attitude of 'pure' computer men towards their female counterparts doing the messy work was intensified to a quite extraordinary degree in their attitudes towards end-users. It was embodied in such references to them as 'peasants' and 'Joe Blockhead' and the suggestion that 'we literally kick [*sic*] the users off the machine'. These derisory references were made whether the end-users were women or one of the small number of men, so the ethos was not directly a sexist one in which men disparage women. To a limited extent, the female programmers went along with this attitude. While this is not direct sexism, this type of reference or remark serves to reinforce the present power structure. It re-emphasizes the importance of computer technology outside the computing department and, in doing that, it further strengthens the position of a department that embodies the masculine self-image referred to in Chapter 4.

This elitist attitude was reflected in the way male programmers related to users. For example, I only ever once heard a truly sympathetic discussion, led by men, about the user interface for clerks (who at that time formed the bulk of end-users) on the number of key-strokes they might have to perform, the layout of the key-board and so on. Other conversations which did occur in my hearing on this subject were superficial. The one set of users for whom this was not true were the busy consultants in the Intensive Therapy Unit and Accident & Emergency. Much effort and time went into designing sophisticated user-interfaces for the hectic atmosphere in these high profile departments. But these were the senior people and all male, not the low status, largely female, clerks.

There was a tendency amongst some men, anxious to move on to the next task, not to stay with users and watch them working. They didn't ask in a meaningful way if the user interface was satisfactory and didn't sit and discuss alternatives with them. I am aware that there are counter examples to this generalisation as there are to other generalisations I have made. But they are true of most men and, most importantly, they are true of the men who set the tone, who control the machinery and who have the highest profile. They are impatient to move on to the next job where they can use glamorous, state-of-the-art techniques, the kind of work which will bring them promotion.

This reluctance of men to spend time with women end-users, fine-tuning their systems, was facilitated by the women end-users' lack of confidence in their ability to use even a fairly simple system. They felt little inclination to voice their doubts about, say, the efficacy of the system. In doing so they would leave themselves open to being humiliated by their apparent lack of knowledge. There was always a tendency for them to feel that the men knew best because they knew about computing and women did not. Once a man has sensed a woman's lack of confidence and low self-esteem in computing matters, he takes advantage of them and is encouraged by her deference to become master of the situation.

Some men did listen attentively. But their colleagues kept their distance from them and would be unlikely to seek advice on computing matters from them – they ended up lower in the 'pecking order'.

Women, on the other hand, tended to sit with the clerks who input data and, not only did they observe how their system operated, but also could see other jobs being done manually – jobs which lent themselves to being quickly computerised. As we shall see later, supplying what clerks really want is a messy, nurturing job which men feel little obligation to do.

## Human Settings

There are three main ways in which programmers or systems analysts (these are different job titles sometimes used for the same task) need to listen to end-users. One is ascertaining the end-users' requirements in the form of an initial system specification. Men are generally willing and competent at this task; this phase is often fun! The second we have just discussed – fine-tuning user interfaces and so on.

The third is being sensitive to the 'existing human settings: physical, organizational and sociocultural' (Kramer and Lehman 1990, p166) into which the new computer system is to be fitted. No new system is introduced into the equivalent of a green field site. The people who will be using the system will have varying levels of understanding of computing and all sorts of pre-conceptions and attitudes. Some will be keen but others full of fears and foreboding, including the worry that they will lose control if their department is computerised or a radically new set of procedures is introduced.

Programmers who feel most at home in a world of pure computing would prefer a green field site, one without 'messy' human emotions and foibles. They see their job as getting a system up and running and not as persuading, educating, encouraging and, if necessary, counselling the apprehensive end-user. Male programmers do to some extent acknowledge the emotions and fears of these people but their response to them is superficial; they do not really enter into their frame of reference. It is not sufficient for a programmer to make paternalistic gestures and tell the end-user 'not to worry', implying that they know best and, if the end-user would only trust them, all will work out well in the end.

In one notable instance this 'we know best' outlook resulted in a system being scrapped. The responsibility for developing a system for one of the medical departments was given to a (female) student whom I supervised. Discussions had been initiated by a senior male member of the computing department before the student and I arrived on the scene. His initial contact had caused some upset in that he had been somewhat brusque and reluctant to listen to and understand the attitudes and relationships in the user department. Instead he marched in with a 'we know best' outlook and, at least partly as a result of this, there was antipathy on the part of the senior management in the medical department towards the introduction of a new system. All in all, we were not working on very fertile ground. So, although we spent almost six months writing a system which we thought worked, we failed to regain the confidence of the senior medical staff of that department. Consequently we failed to gain the co-operation of the more junior staff in working through the details of how their requirements might be met.

Eventually the development was abandoned because not enough thought was put into the 'existing human settings'. No sympathetic discussion occurred about the need to convince this department of the advantages of a new system, nor was there discussion about ways of approaching staff who were fearful of computers. Had that exercise taken place at the outset and more sensitive thought been applied to the environment into which we were introducing this new system, we would have stood a better chance of success. It is my hypothesis that many women would have made this more sensitive approach, something which the 'men from the microworlds' find difficult.

At present, women are much more aware than men of the need to accommodate 'existing human settings'. This is a good example of what I asserted as part of optimal feminism, namely that because of their upbringing, women bring a more sensitive, nurturing attitude to their work. But this is not an argument for replacing men with women. In the longer term men should be brought up to have a similar nurturing, caring attitude and should be sensitised to this important dimension of their work. At the same time the task of accommodating existing human settings should be awarded more kudos. This is essentially part of what I call later in this book the *liberal* level of change.

# 6

# 'We'll Teach You to Go into Computing!'

> *... people are little aware, when a boy is differently brought up, how early the notion of his inherent superiority to a girl arises in his mind; how it grows with his growth and strengthens with his strength; how it is inoculated by one schoolboy upon another ... and how sublime and sultan-like a sense of superiority he feels ...* John Stuart Mill 1869 (Mill 1984, p324)

What happens if you are female and at school, still quite young, you haven't yet taken your GCSEs[1], and you develop a taste for computing and start wondering about a career in, amongst other things, IT? First, I shall show how things start off in a reasonably equitable way for boys and girls at school level and then progressively deteriorate, as far as the girls are concerned, as they move from schools into the universities.

The deterioration starts in schools and continues into higher education. Universities play a dual role in their influence on students: first, obviously, as teaching institutions where the content of the subject is taught; secondly, the ethos that pervades them must influence students' perception of the subject. If, for example, and as we shall see is in fact the case, the subject at higher education level is taught almost entirely by men, then it is likely to remain a subject for men. Women are likely only to be allowed in as 'guests'; they are merely tolerated provided, of course, they continue to do things the 'right' way. This encourages the philosophy that computing is a man's world where women are second class citizens. This is an attitude which they will take with them into their work in industry and commerce, reinforcing men's predominance. Moreover, most teachers of computing at secondary and higher levels will have been through this formative process and will carry this attitude of male dominance into the classroom.

---

[1] As already explained in Chapter 1, the General Certificate of Education is an exam normally taken by 16 year olds in most of the UK. 'A' or Advanced level is taken 2 years later.

After discussing the lot of girls and women at schools and in the universities, I examine the academic profession, how you can get into it and once in it, get promoted – if you are a man, that is.

## 6.1   Secondary Education

### Some Facts

In the typical year of 1990, 40% of attempts at GCSE computer studies were made by girls, who accounted for just over 40% of successes. So the beginning looks promising; the difference between the number of boys and girls attempting the subject and the difference in their success rates seems fairly small at this level.

Staying with the same national cohort and moving on to 'A' level computer studies taken at school two years later, the situation has already started to deteriorate. Only 17% of those attempting and 16% of those passing this examination are female. The proportion of females has already dropped dramatically. (See Appendix A.1, p147.)

### Why?

What can explain such a dramatic fall? In the past girls did well at GCSE computer studies in spite of having (as we saw in Chapter 2) all the loading of the computer games and the computer culture in general in favour of the boys. (I say 'in the past' because computer studies is no longer taught and examined by itself at this level.) One would have expected girls' success at GCSE level to encourage them to pursue 'A' level studies in computing, but not many do. This is in spite of the well-known vocational advantages of qualifications in computing and IT. It seems some fairly powerful influences may be at work here. Among them are the influence of ideas about mathematics, the attitudes of boys, the attitudes of teachers and the content of the curriculum.

### The Influence of Mathematics

Historically, computers were developed by mathematicians and used for repetitive 'mechanical' work, often 'number-crunching'; for example, Charles Babbage developed his Difference Engine in the early 1800s in part to recalculate astronomical, nautical and logarithmic tables, and during the second world war Alan Turing and his colleagues developed computing techniques in order to decode intelligence data (Hodges 1985). As more computers became available this connection was reflected in the schools where computers were, and still are, often placed in mathematics and science departments (Newton 1991). And, in universities, computer science departments often arose out of mathematics departments, not just in the UK, but in other countries too, such as Australia (Clarke and Chambers 1989, p412). A good proportion of these mathematics and computing departments were for many years run jointly – and in the UK a few still are. Lately of course this image has changed and nobody would now deny that computers have a place outside the mathematics department. Indeed the National Curriculum introduced into UK schools in 1994 requires computing to be taught in all subject areas. But until only a few years ago many university computing departments kept 'A' level mathematics as an entrance requirement. The association of computing with mathematics is dying a very slow death.

All this implies that the low numbers of women taking computing at 'A' level and beyond are due, in part, to the fact that they don't like mathematics. Two US studies conducted in the late 1970s (Armstrong 1981) indicate that at the age of 13 girls out-perform boys in some mathematical tests. But by the age of 17, 'math anxiety' is such that girls generally perform below boys on these same tests. Not surprisingly, therefore, girls' attitudes towards mathematics is more negative than that of the boys.

The relevance of this negative attitude of girls towards mathematics is that there is some evidence that students' attitudes to mathematics are correlated with their attitudes to computers. This was a finding of a study of Grade 8 (13 year old) and Grade 12 (17 year old) students in British Columbia (Collis 1987). They were all asked questions about their attitudes towards computers and to mathematics, as well as questions about their use of computers.

The investigators found that a negative attitude towards mathematics was a reasonable basis for predicting a negative attitude towards computers. And this was even more so in the case of females, who were even more likely than the males to associate negative attitudes about mathematics with negative attitudes about computer use. (Incidentally, the converse did not hold. It was more hazardous to predict from a knowledge of a student's attitude towards computing what her or his attitude towards mathematics would be.)

There does appear, therefore, to be some link between attitudes to mathematics and attitudes to computing and, moreover, the link seems to be a directional one from mathematics to computing. So, the educational and cultural ambience is such that girls in their latter years at school lose their confidence in mathematics, have a negative attitude towards it and so, in consequence, a negative attitude towards computing. And while this climate may not influence a woman who is asked to use a word processor at work, it may well influence a woman deciding whether or not to embark on an undergraduate computing course.

My intuitive belief is that girls and women are just as able at maths and computing as boys and men. My experience of teaching women at undergraduate level tends to bear this belief out. Once they get onto our courses, women enjoy and show a facility for the mathematics involved to the same extent as men. But there is an ambience, including a self-perpetuating predominance of men in both subjects as well as the cultures they have developed to maintain that dominance, that progressively lowers the confidence of girls. This is quite probably an important factor in explaining the difference between the number of women and men undergraduates.

There is some doubt as to whether girls are correct in thinking that if they are diffident about their performance in mathematics then that is a reason for their being diffident about their performance in computing. Pamela Kramer and Sheila Lehman found some evidence that 'while all mathematics grades reflected overall grade point average to some degree, none of the mathematics grades significantly predicted success in college-level computer courses' (Kramer and Lehman 1990, p170). Maths and computing should be seen as much less strongly linked in general. Moreover, in this particular context, girls should be taught not to assume that, because maths gives them the shudders, they cannot enjoy and be successful in computing.

## Boys Will be Boys

In Chapter 2 I raised the question of whether schools might redress some of the imbalance against girls created by the informal social processes outside school. But as we noted in that chapter, schools tend to be a microcosm of the larger society and reflect the attitudes of the wider world.

This is nowhere more evident than in the behaviour of boys with regard to computing in schools. Boys in school display the usual domineering behaviour and presumption of privileged access.

Many schools provide opportunities for pupils to 'have a go' at computing outside timetabled classes. In some schools these sessions are organised on a formal basis as 'Computer Clubs'. They may be used for trying out new activities or for providing extra time to complete set tasks. In mixed sex schools boys will dominate these unless action is taken to prevent this. In 151 mixed schools that had computer clubs, only 11 were reported to have equal membership of girls and boys. In 238 schools, girls formed only 19% of those using computers in clubs or other non-class activities. Lorraine Culley reports how girls appeared uncomfortable in this environment and indeed the girls themselves confirmed this: 'The boys considered the computer room to be their "territory" and girls tended to be regarded as "aliens" to be very grudgingly accommodated.' 'We just get told to go away, we get pushed off the computers ... the boys think they own them, they made us feel really uncomfortable ... The boys said they should use them before us'(Culley 1986, pp29–31).

As for the more informal atmosphere of the club, this 'allowed the boys to be even more "pushy" and derogatory about the girls and their work than they could be in formal classes'. Even when girls-only sessions were arranged, the boys reacted badly and Culley observed boys 'continually coming in and interrupting the girls who had also to run the gauntlet of mocking boys on their way into the computing room'. No teacher had observed this, so the girls-only session was almost abandoned because of lack of interest. In one girls-only school, however, there was a well attended and popular club and in another a lack of facilities meant there was no club but nonetheless the girls were keen and a club was to be organised.

In the US where computer camps are more common, boys dominate in just the same way. Three times as many boys as girls enrolled in these summer camps and classes; moreover, the ratio of males to females increased with grade, cost and level of difficulty of the programme (Hess and Miura 1985).

In mixed classes, Culley notes, boys can have virtually complete control over the available computers. Certainly they will go for the newest, most sophisticated machines and girls who try to get access to them will often be elbowed out of the way. During interaction with the teachers boys, because of their greater confidence in and familiarity with computing, consistently ask more questions and make more comments. Indeed girls are often marginalised in a physical as well as a learning sense, finding themselves relegated to groups at the back or sides of the room, reminiscent of the playground and games arcade scenarios I described Chapter 2. Few teachers seem to make any attempt to counteract the boys' dominance and they are much more likely to make more eye contact with boys than girls when referring to technology in general, and computers in particular (Sanders 1990). Sanders also notes that teachers usually choose boys to assist them in the teaching class rather than girls, thus exacerbating rather than improving the situation.

All this is against a background of there being some evidence that girls thrive in co-operative rather than competitive groups (Berge 1987).

## The Teachers and their Attitudes

The fact that few teachers seem to make any attempt to counteract the boys' dominance, indeed many foster it, brings up the issue of teachers' attitudes.

I have already noted the fact that, until recently, in most schools students have been introduced to computers in the context of mathematics and science curricula by mathematics and science teachers. Ominously, there is some evidence that many of these teachers believe that qualifications in technical subjects are less important for girls than they are for boys (Spear 1985).

That science teachers tend to favour boys in this way may be due to the fact that the teachers are predominantly male. Peggy Newton cites some data compiled by Carter (Newton 1991, p146) which shows how male and female school teachers have contrasting attitudes to computers. They differ in how computers should be allocated, what they should be used for and the value of female teachers as role models. Female teachers were found to be more egalitarian in their views, believing that computers should be pervasive and could be used to teach all subjects. Male teachers, on the other hand, took a more elitist view – that priority for access should be given to those of high ability, particularly boys interested in science and mathematics.

On the more general point of equal opportunities (EO), John Pratt, describing a study of secondary school teachers which took place in 1982, reports that women were more likely than men to be sympathetic towards the enactment of equal opportunities policies (Pratt 1985). One striking contrast within this study was the difference between teachers' belief in EO in principle and their commitment to implementation of good practice. But, interestingly, these differences were more apparent among subject specialisms than between the genders. The teachers whose main subject was either English or social studies (the latter mainly male) were in favour of good EO practice and the teachers of maths, physical sciences and technical crafts (all largely male) were least in favour. (So, in spite of Carter, on this view the differing attitudes to EO tended to follow subject specialisms rather than gender.) It is reasonable to suggest that these attitudes will be reflected in attitudes towards access to prestigious subjects like computing and in providing access to computers and all that goes with this.

It is now over ten years since this report was published and, nowadays, teachers would probably be less ready to appear lukewarm about the implementation of good EO practice.

## The National Curriculum

This seems a good point at which to look at changes in the National Curriculum. One major change is that computer studies is no longer an examinable subject in its own right in the GCSE curriculum. It is now taught throughout all subjects and no longer exclusively by maths, science, information systems and computing teachers. So it will be taught also by teachers of other subjects such as English, history, modern languages and social studies. In other words, the emphasis of teaching will be switched from those who, according to Pratt, appear be biased against girls, towards those in favour of good EO practice and this should obviously benefit the girls.

This cross-curricula teaching consists largely of word-processing, spreadsheets and minor database systems, shifting away from programming and software development. Boys as well as girls are likely to be disadvantaged in some ways by these changes. But girls are likely to be more disadvantaged than boys. They come to computing with much lower confidence and much more anxiety than boys. Without the sustained and explicit teaching in programming, they are only too likely to stay at the newly emphasised level of word-processing, spreadsheets and minor database systems. They will shy away from programming. Their involvement with hardware on these terms will confirm even more strongly for girls what computers really are: the modern equivalent of the typewriter, that great symbol of female emancipation.

Defenders of the changes in the National Curriculum point out that IT is compulsory and that it includes handling information, measure and control, applications and effects, modelling and communicating data. The fact is, however, that girls will gravitate to the level at which things are done using off-the-shelf packages; they will not aspire to doing any programming themselves and the small percentage of female 'A' level computing candidates, 17%, is likely to get even smaller.

Another worry about the effect on girls of these changes is that girls come with so little confidence and so much anxiety and negative attitudes towards computers that, if they are to be persuaded to continue with computing, they need to be taught by teachers who are themselves confident, who do not have high anxiety levels about computing and who enjoy it. Such teachers are more likely to be found amongst the specialists who previously taught it. Many of the teachers of other subjects who now share the teaching of computing will not have this enthusiasm for it. Indeed some of them are probably going to be mild, or even in odd cases severe, computerphobics. They are hardly likely to help the girls overcome their anxieties and difficulties. (The boys, on the other hand, with their greater confidence, could well start to bully and taunt these diffident teachers.)

## Girls on their Own

Schools, it seems, only play upon and exacerbate the different levels of confidence between boys and girls and widen yet further the gap between them. Boys, as we have seen, act aggressively and tend to push the girls out and, some would argue, a significant proportion of male teachers of science and mathematics are biased in favour of boys and against girls.

   This raises the question of whether girls should be taught in all-girls' schools and isolated from competition with boys. It is surprising how little the literature deals with this topic. In all the reports I have read and references I have seen on gender and computing in schools, I have found only a handful of papers that discuss this possibly important factor. One of these rare references was in a British study that reported how girls in girls' schools *were* interested in computing. In fact demand was so high that physical and teaching resources were inadequate to meet it. As one teacher put it:

> My experience in girls' schools is that in a work environment not shared by boys, [girls'] behaviour isn't modified by any expectation that girls should be less interested in technical skills than boys. (Culley 1986, p33)

Of course, one swallow does not make a summer, and to give one example of somebody not brought up in the shadow of boys does not prove my intuitive belief that girls and women are just as able at maths and computing as boys and men. But Ada Lovelace (1815–52) is a shining example of such a woman. She played a key role in conceptualising what is sometimes termed the 'first computer', Charles Babbage's Analytical Engine. Ada, Countess of Lovelace, was Lord Byron's daughter. She had an isolated and privileged upbringing and her education was not overshadowed and complicated by the presence of boys. She was able to develop a love of mathematics and her descriptions of Babbage's work

> . . . are remarkable because of her conceptual understanding of the Analytical Engine, when few people recognised its value, and her ability to express that understanding by using apt metaphors and visual examples. Her descriptions of the Analytical Engine can also be used to describe the modern computer . . . defining its limits and its potential. By correctly connecting her conceptual understanding with the context of the Analytical Engine in the development of science and technology, she expressed a vision for the Analytical Engine which still has meaning today. (Toole 1992, p14)

## 6.2   Higher Education

We move on now to higher education, particularly in the United Kingdom. The number of women taking computer studies almost doubled over the five-year period from 1988 to 1992, but this was the doubling of a very small number indeed. While the number of men increased from 4651 to 6570, the number of women increased from 484 to 914, a percentage increase for the women from 9.4% to 12.2%. This is against a background of women in all disciplines now making up nearly one half of the undergraduate population (see Appendix A.2, p148).

Although there was an increase in women taking computer studies over this five-year period, there is evidence that these figures have since dropped and proportionately fewer women are now studying computing. Figures I have collected for individual institutions for 1993/94 range down to a startling 2%.

When I discussed secondary education earlier in this chapter, I gave a picture of the prevailing conditions in which girls at school have to learn computing, including such factors as teachers' attitudes, boys' colonialism and so on. Rather than present the conditions in which women find themselves in higher education in a section on its own, I refer to these conditions as I discuss other topics such as language and the universities' role as employers.

## 6.3   Universities as Employers

This book is concerned with the shortage of women in computing and we shall be looking later at ways to improve the situation. Universities must play a key role in all this. Graduates of universities, male and female, enter industry, commerce and the civil service to fill the higher status computing jobs. The universities also teach those who will be teaching computing and IT in the schools. They are, moreover, the places one would instinctively look to for new ideas. I shall therefore examine in some detail the process of employing and promoting women within these institutions, since this must have a profound influence on the subject and on girls' and young women's view of it.

### The Staff Entrance

Women are few and far between in university computing departments, except of course in the crucial and supportive roles of secretaries and administrative staff which are almost exclusively filled by women. In 1991/92, in 28 institutions that were universities before the 'upgrading' of the former polytechnics, i.e. what are called 'old' universities, the percentage of women in *lower* level teaching and research posts was 13.4%. This figure dropped to 6% at the *senior* levels. To put this another way, only 10.7% of academic staff at *all* levels working in computer science in the sample of 28 departments were female. (See Appendix A.3, p149.) Of the departments I surveyed 18% had *no women academics at all*. In 1991/92 only one computer science department in all the 'old' universities had a female head. This imperceptible presence of women affects not only the image students have of the relationship of women to the subject, but it also influences their view of universities as future employers.[2]

Every university will avow that its employment practices are absolutely fair; jobs are advertised, all candidates are considered equally carefully and no bias occurs in the interviewing process.

Yet somehow the situation remains the same. When challenged, those who do the recruiting and interviewing respond with some justification, 'It's simply that not enough good women come forward. If only they would apply, there's no doubt we would appoint them.'

It is a light in the gloom that, with a female computing undergraduate population of 12.2%, the percentage of women in lower level academic posts is 13.4. So the universities can claim that, if good women come forward they have a good chance of being appointed. What is interesting about this position is the lack of active awareness, even complacency, about the low numbers of undergraduate women. What the universities seem to believe is that it's all right to accept this poor 12.2% of female computing students as a catchment pool for female staff. Having accepted that, all that is incumbent upon them as employers is that they be able to advertise themselves as having an Equal Opportunities policy, are committed to the principle of good practice, treat all applicants equally and occasionally issue pious statements on the subject. It is not incumbent on them as 'objectively thinking scientists', whose primary purpose is the pursuit of excellence, to institute change – that is somebody else's business.

There has to be more pro-active interest on the part of university computing departments to attract women at the undergraduate level and thus to increase the number of good women candidates for lecturerships. Some departments are indeed pro-active in this way and encourage the work of Women into Computing (WiC), for example its computing workshops for schoolgirls[3]. But these departments are

---

[2]Students don't expect there to be female lecturers in computer science. I heard once how a secretary in another department looked up from her work and asked a student how to spell 'Francis'. The student replied that it was normally spelt with an 'i', but there was one man in computer science who insisted on spelling it with an 'e'. The student just assumed that all lecturers in computer science are men.

[3]Women into Computing is an organisation of women from higher education, schools and industry whose aim is to promote interest in computing activities amongst girls and women. One particular target is to increase the number of women taking computer studies in universities.

the exception rather than the rule. Indeed for each department that encourages WiC activities there are others that do not; some, in fact, to some extent deter it. A WiC conference, for example, did not warrant inclusion in one department's list of academic conferences hosted by that department.

There are, of course, a number of powerful incentives for not being pro-active about this. Assuming equality of opportunity once appointed, keeping women out reduces the competition for promotion for those who are employed. This is against an ideological background in which a department that even began to approach a figure of 50% female appointments would be deemed to have let 'too many' women in – even if 50% of undergraduates were women. It would be letting the side down and, as a consequence, would be regarded with suspicion by other institutions. The fear of being labelled as 'weak' by having 'given in' to the feminist lobby is a powerful deterrent.

What qualifications and experience are required of candidates for lecturerships? They need to have done well in their first degree, then they need research experience in a reputable institution and in a developing and accepted field. They would normally be expected to have a doctorate or be well on the way to being awarded one and some teaching experience is also considered desirable.

How then do applicants acquire this experience? After obtaining a first degree, the next step is to gain a position to do research – either a paid post such as a research assistantship or a place to conduct research supported by a grant. In either case potential candidates, while they are still undergraduates, have to make themselves noticed, have to put themselves forward. The climate within computer science departments is not one that encourages women to do this. To put themselves forward women need confidence which they generally don't have and which male lecturers do little to foster. On the other hand, these same lecturers often do approach potential male research students suggesting that option and assuring them of their worth. So underlying this pattern of behaviour are pre-conceptions on the part of both staff and students as to what is a 'typical' research student. The result is women are much less likely than their male counterparts to become research students. So there is, for a start, only a limited pool of women candidates and, of these, many will lack the confidence of their male counterparts.

## Climbing the Ladder

Once a woman has gained employment, let us assume she then starts to work for promotion. As we have seen, in 1991/92 only 13.4% of lower level computing academics were women, and only 6.0% of the senior posts were held by them. Thus an already very low proportion is reduced by slightly more than half when we get to the senior posts.

Why are these proportions so different? Some would argue that the 6.0% represents a different and older cohort of women. It is the sort of figure one would expect if this cohort was promoted in proportion to its number but when that number was much smaller. The proportion of women holding senior posts is, the argument continues, still very much less than the 13.4% of women holding junior posts, because the bulk of the women forming the 13.4% are too recently appointed to be within striking distance of promotion. When these women do come within range of promotion, the argument goes on, they too will be promoted *pro rata* and the proportion of senior posts held by women will get closer to 13 or 14%.

This argument is, however, full of holes. For one thing it seems to imply a sudden and recent two-fold increase in the number of women staff whereas, in fact, one would have expected any such increase to have been more gradual. If it was more gradual, one would in turn expect the earlier additions of women to be within striking range of promotion and to be adding now to the proportion of women at the senior level. So, either they have not got their promotion or, if they have, the starting point for the proportion of senior women must have been even more abysmal than the present one.

But in fact there is serious doubt as to whether there has been any increase at all in the proportion of women academics. In my own department in 1985 there were four; by 1990 there were – and still are – only two. If you look at figure A.5 on page 153 you will see that 'the thin black line' at the bottom, which represents women, rose only very gently between 1987 and 1991 and in 1992 it even dropped slightly. This shows just how little of a surge there has been of appointments of women at junior level.


## Teaching

The three areas which count towards promotion are: teaching, research and management/administration. Although, at present, there is no doubt that excellence in research is the dominant criterion, I would like nevertheless to start with teaching.

Many women feel more at ease teaching than they do when engaged in research. But the importance attached to research means that any excellence shown in teaching tends to be devalued. (Is this an example of whatever women work at, men seek to devalue and whatever is devalued men leave women to work at? See page 27.) However, there are moves towards improving the status of teaching and for this there clearly is a need to measure effectiveness. One method increasingly popular amongst employers is to use course evaluation questionnaires or student ratings of instruction (SRIs) to make judgements about teaching performance. But here again women face a problem:

> ... in an academic environment that persistently quantifies all that can be quantified and handily discards the rest women who value teaching should be forewarned that evaluations of teaching performance may be reduced to a single 'average mean' rating derived from student surveys and that those ratings may well reflect a sexist bias (Martin 1984, p484).

A number of variables have been measured in the literature on this subject and I will mention just a few of these: accessibility of teachers outside the classroom for informal contact, the warmth and friendliness of teachers and, finally, self-assurance and professionalism in teaching.

Some research shows (Bennett 1982, Kierstead, D'Agostino and Dill 1988) that students will only rate women highly if they are accessible for informal discussion outside the classroom and are prepared to spend time with students. Male lecturers on the other hand do not have to be accessible to be highly rated. (In both the references cited the gender of the students made no difference to the findings.) While none of the studies or experiments quoted here has specifically tested the computing teaching environment, the availability of staff outside the classroom is as pertinent to the teaching of computer studies as it is to any other subject. Lack of knowledge about a computing language or system can hold students up completely; they cannot proceed at all until information is acquired. Gaining that information promptly from staff is important in order to progress. The implication of this research is that if women are to be judged by their availability and do not make themselves more available than men, then they will suffer penalties in these ratings and hence in promotion. The dilemma is, of course, that if they do make themselves more available than men, this leaves them less time to do the research necessary for promotion.

Diane Kierstead and her colleagues found that to be highly rated female instructors must not only be very competent at factors directly related to teaching, but must also act in accordance with stereotypical expectations of female behaviour. They describe an experiment in which four sets of ten people, five men and five women, were asked to rate two instructors, one male and one female, lecturing on the anatomy of the eye. This was a tape-slide presentation with slides of the instructor shown to the accompaniment of an audio tape. For one set of ten students the slides showed the male instructor smiling, for another he was not, for the third set the woman was shown smiling and for the fourth she was not. The same tape was used for both male instructor's lectures and similarly for the woman's. At the end of the presentation the student subjects were asked to rate the instructors and also provide a list of adjectives describing him or her.

The male instructor in both sets received more favourable ratings than the female instructor (although care had been taken to make the two audio tapes identical in content and as similar in delivery as possible – only the slides showing the instructor varied). The unsmiling male was rated somewhat more favourably than the smiling male and, in both cases, he was considered knowledgable and professional. The smiling woman, although considered 'happy', received fewer adjectives relating to her intellectuality and the unsmiling woman appeared to make little impression with her knowledge.

Again, Sheila Kishler Bennett found that 'students clearly demand a higher standard of formal preparation and organisation from female instructors' and 'women invested considerably in both the formal aspects of teaching and the informal interpersonal aspects of the instructor role in order to earn parity with their male colleagues' (Bennett 1982, p178).

Men can, in fact, afford to be cavalier in their attitude about whether their teaching is understood. A draft questionnaire for students distributed around my department included the question 'Were the lectures easy to understand?' A male colleague responded 'none of our lectures is, or should be, *easy* to understand

... ' Female colleagues don't have the luxury of being able to approach the task of lecturing in this simple frame of mind. Women have to contend also with conflicting expectations of students. On the one hand they are expected to be supportive, nurturing and so on and, on the other, the tradition is that teachers are powerful and authoritative. Elaine Martin illustrates this 'double bind' with a pertinent quotation from a female professor of social science:

> I feel as if I cannot win in the classroom. If I'm organised and 'professional' students perceive me as cold and rejecting. If I'm open and responsive and warm, I seem to be challenged and taken advantage of, perhaps considered not quite as bright (Martin 1984, pp487–8).

The contradictions in this situation are only heightened when a woman teaches a masculine subject to a room (almost) full of men. This is yet another of the many no-win situations that women find themselves in.

I have quoted here situations where women are likely to be disadvantaged by the use of SRIs. As to those measurements where women appear to fare better than men, in Sheila Kishler Bennett's study for example, they reflect situations in which women are perceived by their students as behaving stereotypically and showing warmth and encouragement. The implication is that women must live up to the non-intellectual aspects of behaviour expected of them before they can be rated highly. Men start with an initial advantage over women.

Women have long argued that their teaching skills are undervalued. But student evaluations do not seem to be the answer to the problem of undervaluation. To use these SRIs for promotion creates yet a further danger that women will not be promoted in the same proportions as men. To use them and to allow proportionately more men to be promoted will perpetuate the visible masculine dominance in the discipline and this will, in turn, continue to influence the nature of the subject as it is taught and practised.

Counselling, particularly where mature students are concerned, is an important component of teaching. Behind the scenes in most university departments, not just computing, the need for this is recognised and I hear many reports of female staff doing this work. But, like so many other gendered tasks, while 'very much appreciated', it brings no relief from other departmental responsibilities and no tangible reward. Similarly, remedial teaching for weak students and those with language difficulties is left for women to do whilst men do the 'important' work of lengthening publication lists and bringing in the money.

Even if employers desist from the formal use of these SRIs, all that I have just said is still true. Women still have to handle the double-bind and put much more effort into their teaching in order to achieve reputations comparable with those of their male colleagues.

## Research

A sound record in research is, at present, the sure and certainly the most important way to earn promotion up the academic hierarchy. This record is judged on the sheer number of publications and partly on reputation amongst fellow academics. These publications can either be articles (normally called papers) of varying length but rarely exceeding 30 pages, or other short pieces (see the list on page 153) or they can be books.

## Publications

The criterion used to judge quality is peer review and the requirement that papers be reviewed or refereed by fellow academics is well established. This certainly screens out poor papers as non-publishable and, at the other end of the spectrum, identifies papers of excellence for inclusion in the prestigious journals. This leaves the majority of papers in the middle of the spectrum as publishable in the non-elite journals. So, to some extent, this system does work; it is, however, subject to three faults. One is that authors sometimes use their influence (albeit often unwittingly) to get papers passed by peer review when they should not be. The second is that a great deal of work is published that is worthy only in a dreary way and is probably never read a second time by anyone. The third fault is more important for our present purposes, namely that referees tend to be very conservative and block the publication of papers with unconventional ideological premises, including, of course, papers by feminists.

Leaving aside the question of quality, statistics on publication rates by men and women for 1990/92 gathered from computer science departments in 28 universities indicate that women publish somewhat less than in proportion to their numbers, i.e. less than *pro rata* (see Appendix A.4.1, p153). They published 7.7% of articles, conference papers and contributions to books and wrote 3.0% of books while the proportion of women academics in computing at that time and at all levels was 10.7%. So, whatever the distribution of publications amongst women academics (whether a few publish a lot or these publications are evenly spread) one can reasonably infer they are publishing less than *pro rata*.

The very low percentage of female authors of books is not nearly as significant as it at first appears to be. Although books have a certain glamour about them, the bread and butter of academic publishing in computing, and in other subjects, consists of articles and other short pieces. For instance, in the 1990/92 period the total number of books on computing from the 28 universities I mentioned above was only 34; the total number of articles, etc. was 2040. Most academics gain their promotion by writing articles rather than books.

A lot more information is needed about why women publish less than in proportion to their numbers. Is it because of the extra pastoral load that they are expected to take on? Is it because of the extra child-bearing, child-rearing and general domestic load that many have to dovetail with their paid work to a much greater extent than do the majority of their male colleagues? Or are women deterred by the more gladiatorial aspects of publishing and being criticised? Is it that it is more time consuming and emotionally draining for women than for men to cope with having papers rejected? It would of course be very difficult in even the most carefully targeted research to measure this last point.

As far as the rate at which women are promoted is concerned, it would appear that with 6% of the senior posts held by women the promotion rate is not very far below the proportion, 7.7%, of articles written by women. Of course more research is needed, for instance in the distribution of articles among women, before we can say much about the relationship between promotion and publication rates. It looks as if it might transpire that universities are fair in their promotion policies towards women. But two things are very wrong with the situation and need to be addressed. One is the paucity of women in the very top jobs and the other is the pitifully small scale on which women are employed and promoted in general.

Although 6% of senior academic posts in computing are held by women, they are very sparsely represented at the highest of these levels, professors and heads of department. Only 3.3% of professors were women at the time of my survey and, as I have already noted, there was only one female head of department in all the 'old' universities in the whole of the UK. I heard of another appointment of a woman to a headship of department to take effect in late 1993. But this was to the accompaniment of a remark to the effect that the job was becoming less popular, 'so it wasn't surprising that women were being appointed'. No doubt this has been the background to the appointment of at least one other female head of department since then.

One possible explanation for this phenomenon of promoting so small a number to these levels is tokenism. Adrienne Rich describes this as

> ... the false power which masculine society offers to a few women, on condition that they use it to maintain things as they are, and that they essentially 'think like men'. This is the meaning of female tokenism: that power withheld from the vast majority of women is offered to a few, so that it appears that any 'truly qualified' woman can gain access to leadership, recognition, and reward; hence, that justice based on merit actually prevails (Rich 1987, pp5–6).

The fact remains, that even if the proportion of women promoted roughly matches the publishing they do, all this takes place on a scale four to five times less than it should. And obviously talent is lost to academic computing.

## Management and Administration

In an academic computing department opportunities for exercising management skills are varied. There is management of computing equipment, especially hardware, departmental finances, student courses and research programmes and, of course, overall management embodied in the headship of a department.

Women are given opportunities to develop their management skills far less frequently than men. For the reasons we discussed in Chapter 5 concerned with men's appropriation of and identity with technology, management of computing equipment is rarely handed to women. This is a double disadvantage – equipment is important and to have control over it gives the person concerned a high profile and some influence over all individuals within the department since they cannot function without machines. The second disadvantage lies in the sums of money associated with the purchase of expensive computing equipment. To be seen to handle large sums of money gives an impression of power. The ownership of power through machines and finance leads to the acquisition of yet more power. These arguments about money also apply to those who control departmental finances in general. This perhaps explains the reluctance to hand women either of these two types of administrative job.

Where women are given the opportunity to show and develop their administrative skills, in organising teaching programmes for example, these administrative jobs tend to be of lower status and, when women do these well, they earn less credit than men do. Sexist skill evaluation is at work here again. Men and women may do the same job but at different points in time, but when women do them they are less highly regarded than when the men do them. More patently unacceptable are situations also manifesting this phenomenon, where men and women are simultaneously doing the same job side by side, but the men get more credit than the women even though they do the job equally well.

This sexist skill evaluation seems endemic and there appears to be little sign of any impetus coming from within the university system for change. There is heartening evidence that some professional bodies, notably the British Computer Society (BCS), are aware of and are starting to combat some of these unacceptable practices and attitudes. A policy statement on the education, recruitment and promotion of women generally, not just in academia, was approved by the Council of the BCS in 1994. There is action on computer pornography; for example, in 1993 the Institute of Data Processing Management put out advice to IT managers who find members of their staff involved. The Committee of Vice-Chancellors and Principals, composed of the heads of universities, produced a statement on Equal Opportunities for staff, but there has been little change of substance since its publication in 1990. It remains, too, to see what changes result from the BCS policy statement.

## 6.4   In Summary

In this chapter we have looked at some basic statistics on education and seen how the situation starts off reasonably for girls. Gradually, however, things change and, by the time they leave university as women, numbers have fallen and various forces have squeezed them and their influence out of the discipline. Low numbers are an important contributory factor to maintaining the *status quo*. Those few who are there find themselves so busy trying to hold their own, that self interest and a simple sense of survival ensures that they will not effect any change.

Schools obviously influence the young, but the atmosphere in schools is, in turn, to a large extent determined by what happens in universities. Universities have fairly well dictated the way the subject matter (irrespective of whether or not it is gender biased) is taught in schools. So what happens in universities is important and I have spent some time examining these institutions.

We have looked at the structure of the academic teaching profession and many of the ways in which it appears to act against the interests of women, both those who are within it and those who are influenced by it – particularly students. The ways in which women students and their male peers are influenced is complex and multi-threaded. One of those threads is language: examples, analogies and metaphors. I turn to these in the next chapter to demonstrate their masculine nature and how their influence, though unconscious, is powerful and detrimental to women.

# 7

# Language in Computing:
# 'Careful, Ladies Present!'

> *Language is evidently ... one of the principal instruments or helps of thought; and any imperfection in the instrument, or in the mode of employing it, is confessedly liable, still more than in almost any other art, to confuse and impede the process, and destroy all ground of confidence in the result.* John Stuart Mill 1868 (Mill 1936, p11)

## 7.1   Why Do Mere *Words* Matter So Much?

Many would argue that to make a fuss about language is to tackle only a superficial manifestation of something that is far more deep-rooted than 'mere words'. The opposite point of view is exemplified by the philosopher Wittgenstein for whom language was central to a form of life and who maintained that 'the limits of the language ... mark out the limits of my world.'[1]

Feminist writers vary amongst themselves in their views on language. Dale Spender, perhaps the best-known writer on the influence of language on the position of women and whose book *Man Made Language* is a classic, concurs with Wittgenstein about the all-important role of language:

> Language helps form the limits of our reality. It is our means of ordering, classifying and manipulating the world. It is through language that we become members of a human community, that the world becomes comprehensible and meaningful, that we bring into existence the world in which we live.
>
> Human beings cannot impartially describe the universe because in order to describe it they must first have a classification system. But,

---

[1] This is from Wittgenstein's *Tractatus Logico-Philosophicus* (Wittgenstein 1922). His original German reads 'die Grenzen der Sprache ... die Grenzen meiner Welt bedeuten' 5.62.

paradoxically, once they have that classification system, once they have a language, *they can see only certain arbitrary things* (Spender 1990, 1st ed 1980, pp3 and 139).

This 'man made language' removes the means for women to articulate their experience, leaving them the choice of either internalising male reality and thus alienating themselves or being unable to speak and having to be silent.

This determinism, the view that language, and language alone, determines what one sees and can think about, has been challenged. For instance Deborah Cameron (1985) argues that language is not uniquely powerful in the way that Spender suggests; it is only one amongst the range of social institutions shaping people's ideas and attitudes. And, of course, there is the whole question of how far language is merely symptomatic of people's perceptions and attitudes as distinct from being the cause of them.

Spender's view that women, faced with man made language, are forced into either alienation or silence depends on the premise that there is a very close relationship between thinking and words: one cannot think without the appropriate words and to use the appropriate words is to think. This idea of an indissoluble link between language and thinking has been contested. Many of us have come across men who use gender correct language and yet their deeds belie their words. Their language is neither symptomatic nor causal. Clearly this is an instance where men have been forced to use language that conforms to certain standards and this, in turn, raises the question just how far men do have the control of language which Spender asserts they have.

While I would not argue that language is deterministic in the way that Dale Spender claims, there are occasions when the use – or non-use – of words can be influential. Deborah Cameron points out (p82) how the word 'patriarchy', while often used by feminists, is not used by the media in discussion of women's subordinate role. Its circulation is severely restricted largely because those in charge of the media realize how influential words are. This severely restricted circulation limits the use of a powerful conceptual tool for discussing the *status quo* – it is confined in use to preaching to the converted. 'Patriarchy' neatly encapsulates the present relationship between women and men and we need words like this to characterise this relationship.

On the other hand the word 'feminist' is in frequent use because it still carries pejorative overtones even to otherwise enlightened listeners and readers. If one side, e.g. the patriarchy, can gain control of the meanings and connotations of keywords like these, they do much to tilt the whole debate in their favour.

## 7.2   Computer Language

My own view is that language is of deep and formative importance and therefore we must examine its influence. One source of its influence is the fact that the words we use for concepts convey meanings at different levels and this is as true of computing as elsewhere. One level is the formal meaning, the understanding of which is necessary for computer work. Women in the workplace are as intellectually capable of grasping computing concepts at this level as their male colleagues; once they have been taught the words they understand their meaning. But women and men understand the meaning of these words at another, almost subliminal level, a level that conveys the men's message 'these words mark out our territory, not yours, you do not belong here, you may visit as a guest, you are not a citizen of our world'. Men territorialise women with their words.

Parallel to what happens in the workplace there is every reason to suppose that schoolgirls understand computing language; their performance at GCSE proves they do. Their success rate at 'A' level is as good as that of boys and my experience is that the same is true at degree level. And yet there is a succession of drops in the numbers of females as one moves up these educational levels. Why this turning away from computing, when their intellectual grasp of what is said is clearly adequate to the task? I believe that one very important factor, amongst others, is the non-formal, subliminal connotations of the language used. Again, the message is 'We know that you understand what we are saying at the formal level, but take note of our other message – you do not really belong here.'

## Names and Labels

It isn't just the words used *within* subjects that matter – the words used to label them and to group them with other subjects are also very important. For instance, computing in university prospectuses is usually classed as a science along with subjects like physics, chemistry, biology and electrical engineering. Or it is known as information technology or various branches have acquired the word 'engineering' in their titles.

In case you are wondering 'What's in a name?' it is worth looking at these labels and examining their impact on girls' and women's attitudes to computing. These labels are quite gratuitous; there is no good or logical reason for using them. But as a means of using language to shape people's thinking, this use makes good sense from men's point of view. These words tend to put women off and are part of the process of job-gendering computing at the higher levels. So let us look in turn at the labels 'science' and 'engineering'.

### 'As Scientifically Proven'

As I have noted, computing is frequently classed as a science in university prospectuses, but there is good reason to think that this is a misnomer. Science attempts to explain and predict the world using the experimental method and observation and, on the basis of these, formulating laws and theories.

Computing, however, makes no attempt to explain or predict the world. It may be a useful tool for those who are attempting to explain and predict on other grounds, but that is a different thing.

**Engineering Metaphors**

Computing is taught using metaphors, analogies and examples drawn largely from a male environment. Women students have therefore always been required to understand what they are taught through a screen of male values and experience. This has been highlighted in the last two decades by the large scale importation of engineering terms as much on the software side as the hardware side. Terms such as 'software engineering', 'reverse software engineering' and 'data engineering' are now commonplace. The British Computer Society recognised this trend when it said 'that it can best represent the needs and interests of those working in systems engineering' by securing accreditation from the Engineering Council for all its members as either Chartered Engineer or Incorporated Engineer (BCS 1988).

In some ways the discipline is indeed more akin to technology or engineering than science. For example, a civil or mechanical engineer will have at her or his disposal a body of theoretical knowledge to use in the design of a bridge or engine, and may also wish to test this design in a laboratory. Similarly, computer practitioners perform a theoretical analysis to estimate, say, the time it takes to sort a set of data according to an algorithm; they then test the results of their analysis by writing a program implementing the algorithm and running it with a data set. To take another computing example, knowing the physical characteristics of a disc (speed of rotation, seek time and so on) they estimate the time it takes to perform a set of operations defined in software terms and then test these estimates.

In this respect – theoretical analysis followed by physical testing – the engineering analogy is reasonably sound. In another crucial respect it is not. The dominant image the word 'engineering' evokes is one of manipulating and realigning matter (e.g. metals and concrete) and physical forces (e.g. gravity and electricity) to achieve a desired physical end – a bridge or an engine that works. In other words, technology and engineering typically produce artefacts.

The word 'artefact' is used to refer to something that is made, artificial (as distinct from occurring naturally) and which paradigmatically is tangible. Computing can certainly produce tangible objects, for example, pictures; computer controlled robots assist in automobile production. Some claim that software is an artefact too. Certainly, it would be wrong to be inflexible in the use of the word 'artefact' and there are things like light-shows that are not tangible and yet can be thought of as artefacts. And virtual reality displays can in turn be compared with light-shows. But to describe *software* as an artefact seems to be stretching the word too much. Software is a set of instructions with the same sort of relationship to artefacts as a recipe in a cookery book has to the meal that can result from following it.

This stretching of the meaning of 'artefact' seems to me to be an attempt to facilitate the classification of computing as a technology and type of engineering. Once this classification is accepted, then computing is firmly locked into the world of technology and thereby the male domain. Once acquired by men for themselves, the desire not to offend men will prevent women from trespassing.

As Stella Harding says (Harding 1993, p10) this use of the word 'engineering' is a metaphor and she suggests that it is all part of an attempt to professionalise the subject with a masculine bias – part of the process of what I called in Chapter 1 'job-gendering'.

While girls can be presented with the distinction between hardware and software and can understand that software engineering does not involve soldering irons and screwdrivers, the word 'engineering' is bound to shape their image of the subject. Traditionally they feel no affinity with engineering and have always tended to be alienated by it. However much the distinction between hardware and software is stressed, the practice of using the word 'engineering' in the context of computing is like a marketing executive insisting on calling a product by a name that has consistently put off half the potential market generation after generation. It is as if, when targeting a potential male market with a car one of whose selling points is a large boot, they persisted in calling it a 'Ford Shopper'. Something analogous to the care and resources that are devoted to research in these matters in the world of marketing could surely be used to examine the effects of these engineering terms on girls and women.

There really is no intellectual justification for using words like 'science' and 'engineering' when referring to the use of computers. Admittedly it is not easy to find terms to substitute for those currently in use, but this is not why they are so commonly used. One obvious reason is to cash in on the established prestige of science and engineering. But another, less obvious but nonetheless powerful reason, is that they put women off and help to mark out computing as predominantly male territory.[2]

## Toolkits

Words alluding to the paraphernalia of engineering – 'tools', 'toolboxes', 'toolkits', 'workbenches' and other engineering terms are now in regular use in the lecture room and the laboratory. It can be argued that 'tool' need not necessarily imply, or conjure up a picture of, a tool traditionally used by a male. It could just as well mean 'sewing tool', 'kitchen tool' or 'household cleaning tool' – it is up to the listener to interpret it in her or his own way. The trouble is that, when the word is used by somebody whose experiences are evidently not the same as the female listener's and when she is subconsciously aware that all those around her are thinking in terms of screwdrivers and hammers, she will not make the effort to find her own images. Indeed the word 'tool' is systematically used by men in their activities[3]; the implements used in the kitchen are more readily called utensils rather than tools. Cynthia Cockburn writes that the conventional view is that 'Normally, women use utensils and implements – the dishwasher, vacuum cleaner, car'(Cockburn 1985, p220). She continues by pointing out that 'The utensils and implements are . . . tools'.

---

[2] The Engineering Council invites its members and suitably qualified members of the BCS to purchase a range of goods 'EXCLUSIVELY for sale to its registrants' (their emphasis). Men's ties dominate the advertising leaflet. Much of the range – cuff links, tie pins, hip-wallets – are designed for men. Ominously the order form gives as example of titles 'Mr, Miss, Dr, EurIng, etc.'. Surely, if they must use titles, they can admit to the existence of married women among their registrants.

[3] Even to the extent of 'tool' being slang for 'penis'.

To talk of tools, toolkits, etc. is systematically reminiscent of male activity.[4]

Similar arguments apply to 'workbenches'. A workbench evokes an image of a (man's) shelf covered in screws and sawdust with perhaps a vice attached to one edge and with a rack of tools hanging above. A workbench that looks like that is not something that I have ever imagined myself using, I have never thought in terms of taking down the various tools and using them to fashion wood or metal. On the other hand, I have a very clear understanding of what it means to rummage in my kitchen drawer for the cooking utensil that I need. For me, such an image is more easily assimilated. The images created for me by 'workbenches' and 'toolkits' serve to create an alien, if not hostile, intellectual environment.

Is it possible that this emphasis on engineering and other masculine activities arises because computing, particularly programming and such software activities, are in fact not 'manly' enough? Do these terms to some extent compensate for the absence of the screwdriver, the soldering iron and the oily rag – even maybe the roar of engines?[5]

### 'Housekeeping' – A Counter Example?

Terms like 'disk housekeeping' and 'garbage collection' are ostensibly counter examples to the idea that computing is dominated by masculine metaphors and analogies. On closer inspection these turn out not to be counter examples but other examples to support the contention. 'Disk housekeeping' takes place after the primary work has been done – usually amending programs or data. It means maintaining the files on a disk in good order, deleting unwanted files and making back-up copies. 'Garbage collection' is a programmable activity which, strictly speaking, does not remove unwanted data but releases space, e.g. on a disk, that is unused but otherwise inaccessible.

Both terms refer to secondary activities that take place as a result of work on the primary tasks. These activities with names derived from the domestic scene refer to tidying up operations that take place once the 'real work' has been done. It is reminiscent of the housewife and mother tidying up the mess left by the family she serves.

### Rape Metaphors

Continuing the theme of language in general and metaphor in particular, four hundred years ago Francis Bacon produced the following metaphor for scientific investigation:

> For you have but to follow and as it were hound nature in her wanderings, and you will be able when you like to lead and drive her afterward to the same place again . . . Neither ought a man to make

---

[4] This is consistent with some women preferring a piece of equipment if they perceive it as a tool, as opposed to experiencing it as a machine which imposes its own rhythm and rules on those who work with it. See page 21.

[5] Whatever the truth of this, a colleague has told me of an essay by a male student arguing that the computer has replaced the motorbike as a male symbol of masculinity.

scruple of entering and penetrating into these holes and corners when
the inquisition of truth is his whole object (Bacon 1870).

Bacon's rape metaphors helped to shape the methodology of science powerfully
in the past. But of course, it might be argued, these are not now relevant in
methodological discussions. Quotations such as this are no longer directed at girls
and women as they learn technology.

But look a little closer. Although the notion of rape itself may have disappeared,
the language and imagery of male-dominated sex and violence still persists in
computing jargon and must influence girls and women, particularly as they start to
learn the subject. Janet Spavold (1990) reminds us that in literature imagery is used
to suggest a wider range of meanings than that implied by the primary meaning of
the words. Poetry in particular gains a great deal of its power from the undertones
and overtones of words in addition to their straight meaning. In the light of this,
Spavold cites words like: 'violation', 'degradation', 'chaining', 'abort', 'kill' and
'execute'. I even hear colleagues talk of 'squirting data'. The question then arises:
What connotations do these words have for female students? 'Abort' may only
mean the early termination of a program; on the other hand, it could equally well
have the connotation of the abortion of a foetus. We have good reason to suspect
that the image that will be created will be antithetical to feminine sensitivities. The
language and imagery of male dominated sex and violence is as virulent as ever. A
colleague who asked if there weren't any more recent examples than Francis Bacon
which could be included here had himself come fairly close to providing one only
a few days before by telling us he was intending to come round to each of us 'to
extract papers with forceps, if necessary'.

'Divide-and-conquer' is a technique commonly suggested for problem solving in which a solution is arrived at by repeatedly solving problems a fraction of the size of the original. This is partly a violent metaphor, 'conquer', but is also redolent of 'divide-and-rule' which describes an aggressive and destructive style of management that is generally perceived as masculine.

It would be a pity to end this section without a particularly telling example of how the male standpoint is the dominant one. A candidate for a post of lecturer was describing his research into neural networks and the computer simulation of animal behaviour. He talked of how the hoverfly exhibits vision behaviour similar to the corresponding activity in humans and, moreover, its eye is amenable to simulation. The primary purpose of this study was to simulate the activity in the nervous system of the fly once it had located its target. The target in this case was a female and the purpose of tracking it was to mate with it. Here again we are presented with predatory male activity and male sexual dominance as an integral part of research activity.[6]

Women's reaction to this is to retreat, both metaphorically and literally. Metaphorically they 'retire' in that they will not feel comfortable asking questions or getting involved in any consequent discussion. They would prefer to distance themselves from such predatory examples; they fear looking unseemly and over-interested in sex if they were to initiate or get heavily involved in a discussion. Excluded from discussions and argument and keen to progress in some career, they retreat literally to find another more amenable context in which to work.

## Prestige or Power?

I have already noted how intellectually gratuitous it is to import the word 'engineering' into computing. Much the same can be said of the word 'technology' as in 'Information Technology'. I have raised the question of the motive for this. Of course one reason for using these words in this context is to hijack the prestige of engineering (just as so many advertisers hijack the prestige of science by advertising their products as having been 'scientifically tested'); but this is only part, and moreover a small and superficial part, of the explanation. At a deeper level, and one of which men themselves are not aware, the explanation could still be Baconian. This view of science, and therefore also of applied science and engineering, is quite explicitly couched in terms of male aggression and control – witness for example the rape metaphor I have just cited and a further sequence of examples of this underlying attitude that are given in Chapter 12. Could it not be that the use of words like 'engineering' keeps alive at an unconscious level this masculine view which emerges up to the conscious level in the Neo-Baconian talk of 'abort', 'slave', 'kill' and 'forceps'? No wonder women 'hear' the men's message, 'This is our world, not yours!'.[7]

---

[6] It is interesting to speculate whether the reaction would have been as favourable if a female candidate had given a presentation which used the predatory sexual behaviour of some species of female spider as its basis.

[7] Even the names of degrees awarded to people, both men and women, for studying the subject are masculine: Master of Science obviously so. Bachelor in this context is perhaps equally masculine. One view is that it

## 7.3   Examples for Practical Assignments

What about examples (as distinct from metaphors and analogies) used for practical assignments, exam questions and so on? In the context of this discussion we can identify three types of examples: those which draw on typical 'male' experiences; those which draw on typical 'female' experiences; and those which draw on the experiences of both groups. A number of examples fall into the last, mixed, category, for instance mathematical examples, sorting employee records and throwing dice. Some fall into the male category. A very few fall into the category drawing on female experiences but these are greatly outnumbered by those from the male oriented category, often metal parts, or, more precisely, washers, screws and widgets and the suppliers of these parts. They are football teams of all varieties, the World Cup or cars. These examples, like toolboxes and toolkits, all help to create a pattern of imagery and thinking in which most women feel outsiders and uncomfortable. Many authors provide lists of names which are mixed but, in fact, the single female name is tacked on to a list of male names. For example: John, Harry, Sid and Liz (Gray 1984).

   Naturally when looking for exam questions or practical examples it is easier to find examples from areas related to one's own background and experiences. So the fact that men produce so many masculine examples need not mean, it could be argued, that they are trying to drive women out of computing or send any other messages. There is clearly some force in this argument, but one's suspicion that there is an underlying message is sustained by the fact that if women draw on their backgrounds for examples this is frequently frowned upon and even mocked. For instance I sometimes base a case study exercise for Master's students on my ideas for *Bytes*. And, although it will be vehemently denied, I experience from some colleagues but by no means all, some disdain for choosing what I suspect they think of as a very 'odd' example – one which they hope will quietly disappear as something unworthy of a 'real' computer science department.

   There are, moreover, some gender-biased examples which can be construed as sexist in that they are hostile to and diminishing of women. Two typical examples used in logic run: 'Jim wants to marry a blond' (Lavington 1985), and 'All women are feather-brained'. The first example serves to reinforce the notion of the dominant role of the male in personal relationships. Man is the subject who does things to woman, the object: it is the man who chooses the woman, not the other way round and, moreover, on the basis of her hair colour rather than any more substantial attribute.

   Some would say that objecting to examples like these is itself a good example of extremist thinking that creates issues and problems where none exist; to use these examples is just a harmless piece of fun to lighten the proceedings. That it is not a harmless piece of fun is shown by putting the second example in terms of race

---

derives from the mediaeval term for a young knight or novice in arms (from the French *bas chevalier*?) a young man who would be both inexperienced and quite likely unmarried; hence perhaps both the academic title and the meaning 'unmarried man'. And the original meaning of the word 'Doctor' was 'one skilled in, and therefore competent to teach, any branch of knowledge; an eminently learned man' (Shorter Oxford Dictionary).

rather than gender: 'All blacks are feather-brained.' This would surely make any reasonable person feel uncomfortable and repeated use of such examples would hardly encourage black people to take up the subject.

## 7.4   It's not Just the Words

The language used in computing does at the least arouse suspicions as to men's motives. This language in the context of the examples and analogies provides strong support for the view that their motives, conscious or unconscious, are suspect and have much to do with male control and domination. Can you imagine this vocabulary and these examples persisting in a world in which women dominated?

# 8

# What Chance New Ideas?

*Women who read, much more women who write, are, in the existing constitution of things, a contradiction and a disturbing element ...* John Stuart Mill 1869 (Mill 1984, p282)

What hope is there then for change? New ideas and research must play an important part in change, but one striking feature of the present situation as far as women and computing is concerned is the shortage of readily available and easily understood feminist writing on the subject.

Those outside universities might reasonably expect them to be a rich source of feminist literature – after all, they are supposed to have a tradition of freedom of thought and the debating of new ideas. Political or financial considerations may affect the work of industry, commerce and the civil service but surely, it may be thought, the universities can conduct research and discussion independently of these influences.

The pretence that the pursuit of scientific and computing research is untouched by political or financial considerations was jettisoned long ago by those within the university system. Some researchers may investigate their subject for their love of it, but whatever their motives, research in the sciences and computing needs money and the suppliers of that money are constrained by financial and political interests. This, in turn, limits the research topics that are acceptable. We saw in Chapter 5 that as work moved from a 'pure' centre outwards towards the messy and untidy, it was less valued. In this chapter we shall see that a parallel phenomenon applies to research in computing. As one moves out of an acceptable area towards such 'impure' topics as feminism, research is not only not valued, it is positively discouraged.

## 8.1   The Motivation for Research

In order to succeed, applications for funds from industry to support research in universities must bring with them the expectation of some financial return to potential sponsors. Occasionally funds are awarded for projects with no obvious immediate return but, even here, there has to be a probable long-term benefit. Funds will only be allocated for conventional developments, for the continuation and improvement of present economic and social arrangements – for increasing the cost-effectiveness of transport, leisure activities, armaments, town planning, weather forecasting, medical care, education and so on. I cited a good example of this type of research topic in Chapter 3 when discussing teleworking. Firms such as British Telecom are willing to invest considerable sums of money in a project that is potentially very profitable to them and which evidently does not upset the established order of things. For a relatively enlightened company like British Telecom the focus is on short-term benefits for teleworkers (who will be mainly women) and on making their immediate working life as comfortable as possible – there is also of course the potential saving on overhead costs, like offices, for example. But the longer-term prospects for promotion, for example, are scarcely addressed and many of these women will still be doing two jobs. Further, and most importantly, housework is still done for free.

Any research project that looks like upsetting present economic and social arrangements is not only itself not going to attract funding, but may endanger funding for existing and other future, conventional, research projects. Feminist research is a prime example of such an unconventional, 'subversive', 'revolutionary' project.

As in all these cases there is no actual threat, but the fear just as effectively leads people to behave as if there were one. When I started work on this book, I was asked by a colleague if I felt no conflict between my feminist research on the one hand and my duty and loyalty to my department on the other. He suggested that, if I persisted with my work, the department's research rating might be in danger of being downgraded by research reviewers and hence its ability to attract funds reduced. This might mean more teaching for my colleagues, less research for them and hence, he intimated, slower promotion. To pursue this work would be to act selfishly. The implication was that my research would not merely be improper but would have a negative effect; the reaction of assessors would very likely be punitive.[1]

## 8.2   Feminist Literature – Supply & Demand

Publication of books and articles is critical for the development and dissemination of new ideas. We saw in Chapter 6 how only a small proportion of books and articles about computing are written by women. (More detail on this can be found in table A.4 in Appendix A.4.) While these figures reflect mainly the proportion of women active in the subject, the presence of only a few female authors does not encourage women to perceive it as *their* subject. Often these female authors

---

[1] The atmosphere is one of rumour and sometimes perhaps over-caution. For example, some senior academics express the fear that major pharmaceutical foundations might withdraw funds from individual universities if they engage in research into alternative medicine.

are the 'successful' token women with whom the 'ordinary' woman is unlikely to identify. The style and provenance of the literature therefore does not encourage the germination and growth of the 'ordinary' woman's own ideas.

Those women who do develop their own ideas might well find themselves attracted to a 'humanistic' rather than a feminist approach. That is to say they might write about situations and developments as they affect the welfare of both genders rather than addressing only the welfare of women. Shoshana Zuboff in *The Age of the Smart Machine* (Zuboff 1988) writes about the perceptions of all types of worker of their work as it becomes increasingly automated. She writes of the difficulties they encounter in doing their jobs in new ways and new environments, for example isolation from fellow workers and a lack of physical contact with machinery and product for plant workers.

Although her observations are not weighted towards one gender, women can sympathise with this approach. But the literature written, either by women or men, from a point of view with which women can sympathise is sparse even in areas where one could reasonably expect to find it.

For instance, authors of computer textbooks on systems analysis and design, while keen to analyse a variety of problems facing implementors, seem coy about discussing and analysing power relations between the genders in depth. Yet I have already described situations in which power struggles could arise – for example, when jobs in computing become segregated along gender lines with women holding the lower status jobs. These situations are, in fact, endemic and important and yet no-one seems willing to address them.

Let me take just one example. Leslie Willcocks and David Mason in a book entitled *Computerising Work*, argue for an approach to introducing computer systems similar to that implied by taking account of 'existing human settings' (see page 66). They suggest that

> ... all projects require a preliminary behavioural analysis that operates on group, coalition, organisational and environmental levels, as well as the level of the individual employee (Willcocks and Marsh 1987, p41).

This proposal is set in the context of a comprehensive discussion of sources of power, conflicts of power and power-sharing within the computing workplace. Various groups among whom power struggles can occur are identified as well as their relationships, but power struggles and conflict between the genders are never mentioned. There is a short section on equal opportunities which identifies the shortage of women and some aspects of job segregation along gender lines. But this discussion of women (and race) is confined to three pages (pp64–6). Given the extensive discussion of power relations between, for example, work groups (computer staff and users) and between interest groups (unions and management) to omit any discussion of why women occupy the lower status, lower paid jobs is – to say the least – odd.

We have already seen in Chapter 6 how the system of peer review acts as a filter preventing 'unacceptable' ideas being published in the major arena for publications, academic journals. The problems faced by scientists in getting unconventional and, in particular, feminist lines of argument into print are nicely illustrated by an American neuro-scientist, Ruth Bleier (1988). The leading scientific journal *Science* had published articles supporting claims that gender differences in brain morphology and cognitive processes do exist. She describes how she submitted an article to *Science* challenging the validity of this and other research on presumed gender differences. As other reviewers had documented, even the existence of such differences is questionable. Ruth Bleier complained in her article for *Science* about the size of samples, the lack of information about the provenance of the samples, unsupportable assumptions and unjustified conclusions. Her article was not published. One reason given was that 'she [Bleier] tends to err in the opposite direction from the researchers whose results and conclusions she criticises', and yet the articles she criticised continued to be published. One could err in the direction of sloppy methods and still be published, but not in the criticism of them.

It would be wrong to suggest that no articles of a feminist cast are ever published. *The Communications of the ACM* (the journal of the US professional computing association, the Association for Computing Machinery) annually commissions the Taulbee Survey; a report of one appeared in 1992 (Gries and Marsh 1992). This is a statistical survey that details the number of women and members of ethnic minorities gaining all types of degree in computing and their subsequent employment. And this same journal has had two special editions on women in computing, one in 1990 and one in 1995. The first contained two articles (CACM 1990) and the second a number of articles describing different aspects of the status of women in computing, largely about women in the US(CACM 1995). But there has been no such publication in any equivalent journal in the UK.

There are rare instances of discussion and analysis of gender issues in the mainstream computing journals, for example an article entitled *Women in AI* appeared in a journal published by what I would regard as male dominated professional association (Strok 1992). Other than this, articles discussing gender issues in computing are limited to sociological, educational or psychological journals and texts. For example, I made a number of references to journals such as *The Journal of Educational Computing Research* and *Computers in Human Behaviour* in chapters 2 and 6 in the discussion of girls' and women's attitudes to computers. But these are not the mainstream influential *computing* journals where the development of hardware and software is discussed.

Proceedings of conferences on women and computing have been published (Lovegrove and Segal 1991, Eriksson, Kitchenham and Tijdens 1991, Adam, Emms, Green and Owen 1994). These conferences, like *The Grace Hopper Celebration of Women in Computing* held in June 1994, are important in that they encourage female computer scientists from academia and industry to discuss amongst themselves technical and social issues. But their readership is the already committed and there is not much risk of preaching to the unconverted as there would be if feminist articles were published in the mainstream journals.

Academic computing journals cover a carefully circumscribed set of sub-disciplines, for example: artificial intelligence, software engineering, neural networks, databases, knowledge engineering, human-computer interface (HCI), programming languages, graphics. A glance through recent issues of a journal such as *Behaviour and Information Technology* which publishes papers on HCI – a subject in which gender differences of approach could prove important – produces no papers on gender. The same is true of *The International Journal of Human-Computer Studies* – which, incidentally, until as recently as the end of 1993 was entitled *The International Journal for Man-Machine Studies*. The day seems a long way off on which all these journals will feature articles on gender analysis as a matter of course.

Some may attribute the lack of supply to low demand. Feminist writing, for instance, seldom finds its way onto undergraduate reading lists. I have seen Jeff Hearn's *The Sexuality of Organisation* (Hearn 1989) listed in a reading list for a module in an undergraduate honours degree entitled Project Management. I have also seen Judy Wajcman's *Feminism Confronts Technology* in a module entitled Social Implications of IT; for both of these modules 'gender' appears in the list of topics. But, in spite of these minor but important advances, there still seems to be shyness and timidity about facing the subject in practice – teaching on the topic is pitifully sparse.

The low level of demand must be only a small factor in this situation. The explanation mainly lies on the supply side and has to do with the ubiquitous influence of patriarchy. Patriarchy has always been a characteristic of the older disciplines like physics, maths, chemistry, electronics and engineering where it has largely gone unexamined and unchallenged. It is characteristic also of biological sciences and anthropology, though in these cases it has received more critical attention. It is important that computer science should fall into the latter category and that its patriarchy is examined and challenged.

It is perhaps not too cynical to wonder whether one of the main functions of the present power network is to prevent this examination. Editors of mainstream journals, with a few honourable exceptions, appoint reviewers who, in the present climate, are likely to filter out feminist articles. Publishers tend to appoint men to edit series of books who will do the same. The majority of these are drawn from a pool of senior members of the academic hierarchy, and these are the people who bless or condemn research projects and who, of course, award or withhold promotion accordingly. So even if an author finds a publisher willing to market a feminist book on computing, she or he cannot by any means be sure that it will contribute towards promotion. Consequently any idea of writing such books is stifled at birth.

The Committee of the Conference of Professors and Heads of Computing (CPHC) recently stated in a letter, 'The Committee cannot accept gender related issues as a valid area of research in computing'[2], although there are now signs that this uncompromising attitude may be softening. All this, as we have seen, is under the influence of what industry is or is not willing to tolerate and foster. It would be misguided to hope that the research funding body, the Engineering, Physics and Science Research Council (EPSRC) was some sort of independent force insulated from all this. In fact it is part and parcel of the power structure I have just been describing. The thought of the EPSRC sponsoring a project on computers and the self-cleaning home at the suggestion of a team of women is almost surrealistic.

---

[2] Letter from its Chairman to the Chair of WiC dated 17th June 1994.

# 9

# The Myth of Male Logic and Female Intuition

*I do not know a more signal instance of the blindness with which the world, including the herd of studious men, ignore and pass over all the influences of social circumstances, than their silly depreciation of the intellectual, and silly panegyrics on the moral, nature of women.* John Stuart Mill 1869 (Mill 1984, p321)

## 9.1   Male Intelligence versus Female Intuition?

A basic but unstated premise of all that I have been saying so far is that women are equal in intelligence to men and that therefore, as far as ability is concerned, there ought to be an equal distribution of jobs between the two genders. This would mean having not only equal numbers of women in the top jobs, but also equal numbers of men in more menial, bottom, jobs. This would apply across the board – in computing and in all activity requiring intelligence. Of course, if women were less intelligent than men, then one would not expect an equal distribution of jobs. What a tremendous propaganda coup then, to get men – and women – to accept the idea that, as far as thinking is concerned, there are basic differences which parallel the physical differences between men and women. Men use intelligence; women, on the other hand, use intuition. And parallel to this, men are rational and logical; women are emotional. And so, the myth goes on, intelligence being all that is needed for these top jobs, men are quite right to take the lion's share of them.

Suppose for the moment we think of intuition as the having of a hunch, immediate insight, arriving at a true or, at least, a highly plausible view without consciously stepping through evidence or logical sequences. This is the sort of thing we mean by 'She knew intuitively (or instinctively) that the child was not well'. Perhaps women do think more 'intuitively' than men, though no one seems to have measured this in any rigorous fashion, and it may well be that this phenomenon is more wished for by men than actual. Insofar as men and women do think differently, this need not be something innate in them parallel to differences in their anatomy. It could be explained quite satisfactorily by the different roles women have traditionally been given by society – caring for children and elderly relatives, and so on. These roles have put a premium on developing, to some extent, different and distinct skills.

This of course is treated as if it were a reason for their continuing in these traditional roles. Men, in effect, say 'There is no advantage and no need to apply intellectual processes to working out why a baby is crying; intuitive processes are the most efficient means of answering these questions. This then is the type of work women are made for and they should stick to it and not aspire to high-grade jobs in computing, for example.' The system in this way is self-perpetuating. Men confine women to certain areas of work where they develop certain skills and then claim that the development of these skills shows that women ought to be confined to these areas of work.

Most men who wish to draw this distinction between the way in which men's and women's minds work would make no bones about one being superior to the other (no prizes for guessing which). Others would deny that they are ranking them in this way; the two things are different but equal. It is, however, difficult to believe that the men who talk in terms of 'equal-but-different' really mean what they say; the roles traditionally thought to be appropriate to each way of thinking are strikingly unequal. Both the professor and his wife have been brought up in a society in which being a professor carries more kudos and power than being a housewife and mother. Does he really think that he would not lose out if they swapped roles and he gave up his academic career to bring up the children?

Let us suppose, for the moment, that women are more intuitive than men and men are more intelligent than women. Even so, the only difference in IQ level that it would be plausible to entertain would be that men are, on average, a few IQ points more intelligent than women. If this were established, there would of course be a gross over-reaction on the men's part. Past experience suggests that it would immediately (intuitively?) be taken as an excuse for men holding all the higher-ranking jobs and women having to be content with the lesser ones. This would be to ignore completely the fact that some women are more intelligent than many men, a fact that should be reflected in women holding many senior posts, even if slightly fewer than those held by men.

But having said this, it must be emphasised that in all the very considerable testing of intelligence, especially that of children, there is no evidence of any overall superiority of either gender.

## 9.2   Challenge I: Men use Intuition Too

The idea that intuition is exclusively, or even predominantly, female is such evident nonsense that only those with a vested interest in perpetuating the present distribution of power could believe it. Men in their activities, including the most prestigious professions, use intuition as a vital ingredient.

One difficulty in seeing that men also use intuition is that even feminists have tended to concede too much to the prevailing propaganda by defining 'intuition' in terms of personal relationships and interpersonal dynamics. Joan Cocks, while denying intuition is any kind of sixth sense or emotion confined to women, characterises it as 'a set of reasonable predictions arising from "careful attention to the nuances of personal relationships, from an intelligence trained on the minutely perceptible exterior signs in people around them of loneliness, pride, disappointment, and changes of heart"(Cocks 1984)'(Tong 1989, p133).

The interpersonal area of intuition is obviously an important one and no doubt women excel in it because of their upbringing and training. It is, consequently, easy for men to slide into the conclusion that those things that are important in intuition are a female prerogative. However, important though this area of interpersonal intuition may be, in my view it is too restrictive to confine intuition to emotions and interpersonal relations. Suppose we simply characterise intuition as reaching reasonable hypotheses on the basis of subtle evidence which it is often difficult to pinpoint and articulate. This would of course include 'the minutely perceptible exterior signs in people', but also involves areas completely removed from people's feelings and needs. For instance, a garage mechanic is surely using intuition when he listens to subtle engine noises and senses smells and vibrations and arrives at a hypothesis as to what is wrong with the engine. This long experience of listening to engines might well have started in childhood, just as a woman's focusing on interpersonal relationships might well have started in her childhood. And in both cases this long experience makes their hypotheses valuable. Both are using intuition but, in the case of the garage mechanic, this does not involve people.

The process here is precisely the same as a woman intuiting another person's emotions: evidence which in a formal way is inconclusive and indeed may be difficult even to pinpoint is used almost unconsciously to arrive at a hypothesis. Of course the hypothesis needs checking out by more explicit formal procedures and may, in fact, turn out not to be true. But in the case of an experienced garage mechanic, even if the hunch does turn out to be wrong, it would have been rash not to have tried it out and tested it.

A detective is no more likely than the garage mechanic to call this process intuitive. An experienced detective willingly talks about 'having a hunch' as to who committed the crime. He does not call it 'intuition' – he has learned that is a female trait (sexist skill evaluation?) – but sticks to words like 'hunch' and might well say 'I had a feeling that the butler did it'.

Similarly, what other than intuition, in the way I have defined it, is being used by a doctor who says that diagnosis is as much an art as a science?

Again, what could be more prestigious, even for men, than being at the forefront of scientific research? And yet there is a very influential school of thought that ascribes a pivotal role to intuition in arriving at new hypotheses to be tested. By this view, the accumulation of empirical data does not, by itself, lead to the formulation of new theories; there are no logical and self-conscious rules or steps to new theories. Some kind of creative and imaginative leap is required. Here, of course, one produces the almost compulsory quotation from Einstein: 'A theory can be proved by experiment; but no path leads from experiment to the birth of a theory.' (Storr 1960, p13). To put it another way:

> In contrast to the purely empirical conception according to which
> natural laws can with virtual certainty be derived from the material of
> experience alone, many physicists have recently emphasized anew the
> fact that intuition and the direction of attention play a considerable role
> in the development of the concepts and ideas, generally far transcending
> mere experience, that are necessary for the erection of a system of
> natural laws (that is, a scientific theory) (Jung and Pauli 1955, pp151–2).

To give yet another example, this time from computing itself, the initial steps required in diagnosing computer faults are nearly always intuitive. Few skilled programmers require an explicit error message to tell them whether the fault is a hardware fault, an operating system fault or a fault in an application program. If it is a hardware fault, the computer engineer called out to correct it will use intuitive processes in much the same way as the garage mechanic, not by listening to noises and detecting smells but using 'minutely perceptible exterior signs' not in the people around him, but in machines. The people around the engineer, those who have called him in, will give further verbal clues to assist in the diagnostic process.

If it is a software fault and the programmer believes it to be his or her program that has failed, then, as a start, they will use intuitive processes to locate the error. The data used in these processes include 'exterior signs', for example what output had been made by the program by the time it failed. Only if these intuitive processes fail to diagnose the problem does the programmer have systematically and laboriously to test all possible sources of the fault.

For those with some experience, intuition plays a part in learning to use a new piece of software. Most spreadsheet packages look and behave much the same in spite of apparent differences. While one could read the manual or exhaustively work through the 'help' screens, few of those with any experience do. The experience one has in learning to use other spreadsheet packages permits the use of intuitive learning. You make 'inspired guesses' as to which function key you should use.

Another area in which the application of intuition prevails is in making judgements about probable new developments. Such applications of intuition are used in other spheres as well, but since computing is the subject of this book to illustrate this point using computing is sufficient. In identifying where the leaps in technology and software development are likely to take place and where the most kudos will be found, researchers and academics will use intuitive judgements which are based on their knowledge of the present state of the art, what they read and hear from those they view as their peers. Predicting the next major steps in computing development, hardware and software, requires imaginative leaps just like those needed to predict major changes in science.

My general point is this: Joan Cocks rightly criticizes radical feminists who accept the dichotomy produced by men between male logic and rationality and female intuition and emotion, and who then go on to refuse to have anything to do with the male-appropriated rational side. These radical feminists in this way deprive themselves of far too much, not only in their struggle against patriarchy, but by surrendering their entitlement to take part in rational debate and discussion. One could also argue that men, on the other hand, who accept this dichotomy between male logic and female intuition equally appear to deprive themselves of an asset of immense value. It may take high intelligence and ingenuity to test experimentally some of the implications of Einstein's theories, but surely we reserve the plaudit of 'genius' for Einstein himself and the inspired intuition that led him to form the theories in the first place. If men in their professions, including scientific research, really were confined to the plodding processes of self-conscious step-by-step 'logical' thinking, the world would be a very much poorer place. But they are no more confined to male logic and reason than women are confined to intuition and emotion.

## 9.3   Challenge II: Intuition *is* a Form of Intelligence

Furthermore the whole idea that there is a sharp dichotomy between logic, rationality and intelligence, on the one hand, and intuition and emotion on the other is fundamentally flawed. Perhaps we encourage the belief that there is such a dichotomy by the way in which we sometimes express these intuitive beliefs: 'I feel that she is angry' sounds like 'I feel angry', i.e. the expression of an emotion. But to say that 'I feel that she is angry' is no more the expression of an emotion than is a Chancellor of the Exchequer saying 'I feel it is premature to lower the rate of interest'.

But just to show how deeply flawed the belief in such a dichotomy is, it is worth pointing out that not only is intuition not an emotion, but even emotions have cognitive elements as a logically essential ingredient. You cannot feel guilty without believing, rightly or wrongly, that you have done something wrong; you cannot feel afraid without believing that something, however unspecified, is a threat to your well being. So, far from emotion being some kind of primitive or elemental ache or twinge with no reference to rationality or social context, even simple emotions rely on a whole culture of concepts, norms and beliefs without which they would be impossible. Cocks puts this very well, using the example of resentment:

> . . . while the feeling of resentment is in part an ache of bitterness, it is also a judgment of the action of another as an unmerited wrong to oneself, grounded in a deeper web of at least partially shared and rationally contestable beliefs about what kinds of actions count as injuries rather than as goods. In turn, the expression of resentment is an invitation to intelligible debate over whether the action in question is an instance of undeserved injury or not. If the feeling and expression of passion are tied to reason in such a way, there is no more intellectually subtle form of conversation than that pursuing the connections between context, character, and event, in order to determine what passions

actually were felt and expressed in a given situation and what passions were warranted or at least reasonable under the circumstances. In sum, emotion lies no closer than, say, the logical deduction of conclusion from premises, to some raw animal state (Cocks 1984, p45).

Similarly, and to get back to intuition, to intuit that somebody feels resentment is not to connect oneself empathically to the raw, elemental state of that other person with no reference to socially shared concepts and norms. Obviously the intuition makes as much reference to these culturally shared concepts and norms as does the feeling of resentment itself.

The idea that intuition excludes intelligence is quite clearly false. Intelligence is an integral part of intuition. For example, when I wanted to know why my washing-up machine wouldn't operate this morning, I first established a range of possible reasons – I did not take any action. These options occurred to me only because of my previous experiences with household machines that fail to operate. They were: the machine was mechanically faulty, the water supply had failed, the fuse had gone on the plug or there had been some other failure in the supply of electricity. The last two of these I dismissed using evidence – the 'on' light was on. The idea that the machine wouldn't work because the water tap had been turned off occurred to me as the most likely reason because of my previous experience with household machines that use water and because of the setting of the programme knob – the cycle had started and stopped. I used no direct evidence that the tap wasn't on until I tried to turn it. I used intelligence to establish the options and also to choose one option as a hunch. Thus, for the most part, I did not take deductive or inferential steps – the process was intuitive, but intelligent drawing on past experience played a crucial part in this.

As a young mother I used exactly the same type of procedure to decide what it was that was making my baby cry, drawing up a list of options (hunger, too many clothes, colic, soiled nappies or something more serious) and picking one of them out as my hunch – all of this based on my previous experience of looking after that baby.

In general, the more intelligent and experienced the doctor, the detective, the garage mechanic and the computer engineer, the more valuable their hunches will be. Surely no one suggests that the likelihood of their ideas being accurate has nothing to do with the number of occasions they have encountered similar situations and the intelligence they have brought to bear on them. Intelligence is an integral part of intuition and intuition the predominant form of everyday thinking.

Just as it is misguided to contrast intelligence and intuition, so also it is misguided to contrast rationality with intuition. To assert that intuition is opposed to rationality is to suggest that it is irrational, or at least non-rational, which would include its operating without regard to the evidence or indeed flying in the face of available evidence. But this, as we have seen, is not the case with intuition; hunches are based on experience and, what is more, are checked out and either upheld or rejected in the light of evidence and what are unquestionably rational, logical procedures.

One striking way of underpinning the idea that intuition is an extremely important part of our everyday life and also that it is misguided to contrast intelligence and experience with intuition, is to quote the theory of the brothers Hubert and Stuart Dreyfus as to how the novice becomes an expert. This involves five stages:

1. Novice

2. Advanced Beginner

3. Competence

4. Proficiency

5. Expertise (Dreyfus and Dreyfus 1986, Chapter 1)

### 1. Novice
Novices acquire new skills by means of learned rules and judge their performance by how well they have followed these learned rules. The application of these rules is context-free. That is to say, they are followed regardless of the situation in which they are being applied. For example, rules about driving are applied regardless of whether or not the roads are icy.

### 2. Advanced Beginner
After the novices have had considerable experience in coping with real situations they learn to use more sophisticated rules and also to take into account the situations in which they are applying these rules.

### 3. Competence
With even more experience rules are no longer applied simply because they are applicable but because they will enable the performer to reach a goal. Thus competent performers choose plans and order priorities in ways that will achieve their goals in concrete situations. For example, 'the competent nurse will no longer go from patient to patient in a prescribed order but will assess the urgency of their needs and plan work accordingly' (p26).

### 4. Proficiency
As performers' experience and skill increase they tend to become deeply involved in their tasks and instead of making deliberative, carefully thought-out decisions about how to achieve their goals, they almost effortlessly know what to do in the particular situation and they do this without protracted analysis or decomposing situations and patterns into component features. Dreyfus and Dreyfus call this ability 'intuition'. 'The proficient chess player can recognize a very large repertoire of types of positions. Grasping almost immediately, and without conscious effort, the sense of a position, he sets about calculating a move that best achieves his intuitive plan. He may, for example, know that he should attack, but he must deliberate about how best to do it' (p29).

*5. Expertise*

Experts work so intuitively that their skill has become a part of them and something of which they are hardly aware. Often they cannot articulate reasons behind their judgements. Of course this does not mean that experts are always right, nor does it mean that they cannot check their intuitions deliberatingly 'when time permits and outcomes are crucial' (p31).

I shall return to Dreyfus and Dreyfus in Chapter 12 where I discuss their criticisms of Artificial Intelligence. I shall make the point that they identify intuition too much with 'knowing how' rather than 'knowing that'; as they themselves point out, dictionaries define intuition as a cognitive activity. They also analyse intuition too narrowly in terms of the holistic recognition of patterns experienced in the past. After all, as we have noted, intuition is involved in the production of new ideas in, for example, science where it is not recognition of similarity in old patterns that is required, but a wholly new way of seeing things.

But the Dreyfus brothers are right to say that intuition is not some sort of irrational or emotional thought process. Far from being inferior to more deliberative patterns of thinking, they identify it with expertise and put it at the top of the hierarchy. It is 'the sort of ability we all use all the time as we go about our everyday tasks', something that women can acquire as readily as men. Indeed, as they point out, it is 'an ability that our tradition has acknowledged only in women, usually in interpersonal situations, and has adjudged inferior to masculine rationality' (Dreyfus and Dreyfus 1986, p29). But, as we have noted earlier in this chapter, intuition is not inferior to rationality but complementary to it. Like rationality it is something shared by both genders and something men do themselves a disservice by denying that they have.

## 9.4   'Straight to the Top'?

This idea that men are logical, rational and intelligent and women are by contrast intuitive, non-rational and emotional is a long-standing piece of male propaganda meant to be of general application across the whole range of disciplines, indeed across all intellectual activity. The myth has really come into its own, however, with the rise of computing. Computers have come to 'symbolize the rigidities of pure logic' (Edwards 1990, p105) and, the myth has it, the higher the grade of computing the more linear, rigid and impersonal that logic becomes. After all, the computers themselves work in a logical, linear manner and the more a person thinks in that mode, the more in tune with the machine he or she will be and the worthier to rise to higher levels. But women, so the myth continues, simply do not think in this way. Their cognitive processes are emotional and non-rational, not to say irrational and illogical. It is the men, therefore, with their logical and straight thinking who are in tune with the machines and consequently occupy, as they should, the higher positions.

This myth of the misfit between high level computing and women's cognitive processes obviously serves the men well in their attempts to monopolise the better computing jobs. It must also be one of the main reasons for all but a few women not putting themselves forward for these jobs. Their cognitive self-image is such that they cannot, or will not, think in the required fashion.

This myth involves a tangle of false assumptions and *non sequiturs*. We have already challenged the idea that intuition and rationality are sharply contrasted; we have also refuted the idea that each gender is confined predominantly to one of these modes of thinking; men as well as women think intuitively, and women as well as men think 'rationally' and 'intelligently'.

Let us now turn to another component of this myth. It does not follow that because computers work in a rigid and sequential manner, those who work best with them at the higher grades must also think in this way. In fact there is room for both sequential and non-sequential ways of thinking; indeed they already work side by side in a complementary fashion. In science, as we have seen, there is a need for both the creative intuitive move to new hypotheses and the more mundane sequential checking of these hypotheses. A parallel situation exists in computing. What were once spanking new ideas – such as relational theory, object orientation and functional programming languages – were not arrived at solely by plodding step-by-step procedures. The implementation of them was. The best practitioners are good at both and would certainly gain kudos from the intuitive work. They would also be proficient at implementing their ideas, though they would probably do this by overseeing a number of research students, much as a mediaeval master artist might supervise the productions of his student assistants.

Incidentally, insofar as work at the top involves choosing staff and directing their work productively, here, surely, to the extent that women are intuitive about people, their skill is most at a premium. In the case of very effective female monarchs, some men like to say that they did not rule themselves but merely chose very capable men to serve under them. But as John Stuart Mill pointed out, the ability to choose the right people in such a situation is the key skill (Mill 1970*b*, pp187–9).

The fact that women think intuitively is, therefore, no disadvantage to them and indeed it is precisely at the higher levels that this ability, which the men so foolishly disclaim for themselves, comes into its own.

# Part IV

# What is to be Done?

# Introduction to Part IV

*Now, the most determined depreciator of women will not venture to deny, that when we add the experience of recent times to that of ages past, women, and not a few merely, but many women, have proved themselves capable of everything, perhaps without a single exception, which is done by men, and of doing it successfully and creditably.* John Stuart Mill 1869 (Mill 1984, p300)

We have looked at some criticisms of the present state of affairs as far as women and computing are concerned. We now need to formulate a clearer and more explicit idea of what things should be like – a more complex task than might be apparent from what I have said so far.

The representation of women in higher levels of computing is, like their representation in every other sphere of professional or managerial paid work, scandalously low. It might look, at first sight, as if the solution to this problem would be to make the representation of women equal to that of men and that would be enough. I believe, however, that this is only part of the solution and to see what else might be needed it is important to classify the different criticisms I want to make of the present situation.

To this end I make use of criticisms already made of science and technology by feminists. These are many and varied and somewhat bewildering to the newcomer. However, writers have made some attempt to classify these criticisms[1] and I would like to develop these efforts further, not only to increase the order that has already been suggested, but also to provide a perspective that will generate new ideas. What this final part is concerned with, therefore, is to develop a variant of these classifications.

This is a three-tier classification providing three levels of criticism and solution. The application of these three levels firstly to science and secondly to technology lays the groundwork for their application to the subject of this book – computing. So, I define these three levels and apply them each in turn, though at varying lengths, to science, technology and computing.

At the basic, minimum level there is the under-representation of women in science, technology and computing and the consequent aim of adding more women

---

[1] One of the best-known and most quoted of these classifications is that discussed by (amongst others) Sandra Harding (1986) and (Harding 1991) namely *bad-science* and *science-as-usual*. I am clearly indebted, in what follows, to the style and content of these labels.

to each of these areas without any alteration to their form. This level of criticism and solution is termed *add-more-women*. Of course all you need to generate this level is *minimal feminism*, the belief that women are equal to men in ability and aptitude and that equality of opportunity should be the norm. This, however, is not enough and has to be accompanied by other changes.

The second, or *liberal*, level of criticism demands the application of science, technology and computing for morally worthy ends and for such things as the abolition of unnecessary hierarchies and diffusion of power. It also questions such things as the method of allocation of funds by people who are themselves too involved and self-interested to make objective judgements. Minimal feminism and the policy of adding more women do not generate this set of demands; it is *optimal feminism* that is needed in this case.

Simply to add more women to each of the three worlds or to change the setting in which they are practised really only endorses the *status quo*. The detailed changes which I suggest at the add-more-women level, like attention to language and the naming of concepts, are merely tinkerings with worlds set up by and belonging to men. It is as if all we are doing is to join in the game of soccer, learning its rules and its skills, and getting absorbed in the 'glamour' of soccer, which most of us don't see as glamorous anyway. What we also want is a new game; a game for which we (women) develop the rules; a game which we teach one another to play; a game for which we set the standards; we decide where it should be played and how it should be reported; and we decide what is 'glamorous' and what is not. The development of this new game is consistent with optimal feminism.

This analogy with games is not meant as a narrow analogy concerned merely with computing, but with a whole range of social institutions such as schools, universities, governments, police forces and churches. The men, of course, are going to object; they will say 'These are our games, we invented them and it's up to us to say whether or not the rules can be changed and, if so, in what ways. If you want new games with new rules, then go and invent your own, and stop being a nuisance.'

In some cases, women can set up their own worlds as in girls' schools, women's colleges and indeed the women's technology centres we have today and all these, in some respects, work well. For instance, girls in girls-only schools achieve more than they would in mixed schools. But many of these institutions mimic the equivalent male institutions, for example copying the structure of the much older boys' schools, the wearing of ties and even playing cricket. In fact women's cricket, as played at international level, sums the whole thing up very neatly. It is men's cricket played according to men's rules and nobody pays any attention to it except, like the bearded woman at the fair, as an oddity to gawp at.

So far then, when women have gone off to do their own thing, whether at cricket or in schools, minimum impact has been ensured by their aping the male activity but at a lower level of influence and status. Having said that, if women had devised and used their own rules they would have been derided and mocked and their influence on the worlds outside their own would have been nil. Yet another no-win situation.

But this shows the difficulty of inventing a new game; indeed, in most cases, it is impossible. You cannot have two systems of government at the same level making decisions on the same issues. Nor can you have two systems of law, two distinct police forces nor two sciences. So the parallel of inventing a new game breaks down at this point.

If a parallel game is impossible, does this mean that we have to stick with the game as invented by men? A man would have to be a rabid sexist to suggest that women shouldn't have the vote and shouldn't be allowed to sit in parliament or be prime minister just because men invented democracy. Even men who are moderately chauvinist do not now object to women joining in their games. The disappointment is that, so far, this is all women have done in this context. They have simply entered politics as it always has been played, thereby adding more women, and played the old game according to men's rules.

So what we are looking for is not just the quantitative changes of adding more women at my first level, but qualitative changes at the second, or liberal, level in the aims and methods of science, technology and computing. The third, and radical, level demands not merely changes in personnel or even such things as the uses to which this expertise is put, but change at a deeper level. The main tenet here is that these disciplines are, as currently practised, all inherently masculine. The very essence of the way these subjects are practised is incompatible with the retention of their female identity by those women who engage in them.

Within this radical critique two viewpoints can be distinguished: one of these is that these sciences cannot be made compatible with feminist ideals and therefore should be avoided, a viewpoint I have called *boycott-science*; the other is that there can be changes fundamental enough to bring them into line with feminist ideals and this I call *find-a-new-science* (or, to pursue the analogy of a game, find-a-new-game). For this you do not need to go to *drastic feminism* to find a base. What I am claiming involves *optimal feminism*, the idea that because of their upbringing, women bring a set of attitudes that have great value and strong implications for how one might work in these sciences. These implications are not just about the setting of the activity nor to what use it is put, but the very nature – essence – of the subject concerned.

Chapter 10 is concerned with criticisms and solutions at the very basic, minimum level, that of add-more-women. These solutions include: the explicit encouragement of women to study the disciplines and enter the professions, and the expenditure of effort and money to dispel the myths that some subjects are more appropriate for one gender than another. While the details of change will be different for each of the three fields, the emphasis here, of course, is on changes in computing. Changes at this level simply involve joining in and accepting, without change, the game of soccer.

Chapter 11 deals with the liberal level. Here the solutions will involve changes in the balance of power and a shift of influence away from those who control the purse strings or who have technical know-how towards those with less technical know-how, giving them more responsibility. Changes at this level are about where our radically new game will be played, how it will be reported and about deciding what is, and what is not, 'glamorous'.

In Chapter 12 I examine each of these three areas, science, technology and computing, at the radical level. The Baconian ideals that heralded the birth of modern science are inherently masculine and women engaged in science in its present form have no choice but to compromise their identity. The first radical viewpoint is that these Baconian ideals are incompatible with feminist thinking and therefore we should have nothing to do with them – we should 'boycott-science'. That view can also be held about technology and computing. The alternative to a boycott of these three subject areas is retaining them in a radically different form such that women can work in them without loss of integrity. Science must be practised differently, the development of technology and our approach to it must change. Computing too must change.

In this final chapter I look at feminist approaches to two topics in computing. These are, firstly, programming techniques and the way in which we teach and encourage students of all ages to program. Here the emphasis is on pluralism, that there is not just one right way of doing things; there are many ways of reaching the final objective. Indeed to insist on one right way at the present time is to preserve the patriarchal dominance. Feminist approaches to artificial intelligence, or AI, is the other topic examined in this chapter. There has always been a relatively high number of women interested in AI since its early days and this is possibly why feminists have paid more attention to it than most other computing topics. The basis for AI as currently practised is profoundly masculine and feminists have examined the nature of this masculine basis and discussed some of its ramifications. Such a short treatment of two topics cannot hope to provide the ground rules for a new game but it is hoped that the few ideas that the discussion promotes will at least set people thinking about what a new game might be like.

# 10

# Adding-More-Women

*In all things of any difficulty and importance, those who can do them well are fewer than the need, even with the most unrestricted latitude of choice: and any limitation of the field of selection deprives society of some chances of being served by the competent, without ever saving it from the incompetent.* John Stuart Mill 1869 (Mill 1984, p274)

Very little has been written on possible solutions to the problems women face when trying to make their way in the world of computing. So, one has to turn to other fields for inspiration and guidance on how to proceed – to the already existing analyses of women's role and position in science and technology. Another, more compelling, reason for these preliminary analyses is that many of the ideas that form the foundations for modern science and many of the forces that maintain the momentum of science and technology are relevant to computing.

Let us remind ourselves of the facts – as few as 12 in every hundred jobs at the managerial level in computing are held by women and in senior academic posts the figure is even lower – six in one hundred. In this computing is not that different from other comparable and related fields – some are marginally better (biology, medicine and chemistry), some marginally worse (engineering and electronics) but all are in a regrettable state.

## 10.1  Technology and Add-More-Women

This dearth of women in scientific and technological disciplines is the most obvious and simple criticism and was highlighted by early feminists. So too was the undervaluing, or even denial, of the contribution of the women who were, and are, good practitioners in science and technology. Consequently early feminists sought to identify barriers to women's entry and to provide better access for them. This could be achieved by a range of positive action programmes including examination of the influences on girls at school and their choice of subject at 'A' level and at further and higher education levels.

Early feminists also urged the removal of obstacles to progression for those few women who did manage to enter the profession: relaxing the conventional constraints on promotion; or even introducing programmes of positive discrimination. These policies can be encapsulated in the phrase 'add-more-women'. But, as we shall soon see, this is not a complete solution. It does not, for example, undo the job-gendering whereby science and technology have been made masculine; indeed, involving more women in them in their present form means more women having to compromise themselves. In this sense adding more women worsens rather than improves the situation.

Just how important a component of an overall solution is adding more women? It certainly isn't obvious that adding more women is a sufficient condition for change at other levels, that adding more women guarantees liberal and radical changes. It does not even guarantee that the purely quantitative change at the add-more-women level will be maintained. It might be thought that if significantly more women were added then surely the image of women would change for good. Well, it might. Whether or not it will depends on the reasons for them being there.

For example, in the two world wars the numbers of women working in technological jobs increased dramatically but these changes were a consequence of wartime needs, not the result of the recognition of women's basic rights. Hence, once peace was re-established, regression to the earlier state, where few women worked in such jobs, was easily accomplished.

It is not obvious what the conditions required for a permanent change might be. Even the recognition of the rights of women could be as fleeting as the belief in the justice of highly progressive taxation – who would have thought in the 1970s that the consensus in favour of such taxation, then so strong, would now be so effectively eroded?

The fragility of any change in the right direction is at least partly due to the failure of women to recognise and maintain their rights and the force they could collectively exert. If, almost by accident, they approach this position of equality there is no guarantee on past performance that they will exercise their right to retain it. Women have been, and still are, half the problem.

Paradoxically, success in adding more women would invite the universal reaction of the devaluing of the occupation to which they have been added. For instance, secretaries in the nineteenth century were male and it was then a high status job. Now that it is virtually totally feminised its status is low. The greater the success in adding more women, the more powerful the male backlash is likely to be.

It is plausible to speculate that there could be a critical mass of sufficiently enlightened women in senior positions such that changes in the right direction would become irreversible. Rosabeth Moss Kanter (1977) takes the view that men are more hostile when the minority group of women is small and that such groups need to attain a critical mass of 15% of the total in order to avoid hostility. But this is problematic and more complex than appears at first sight. For one thing it has been found that as the number of women in academic science departments increases, they divide into distinct subgroups that can be at odds with each other. The senior female scientists typically share the values and workstyles of older men and their narrow focus fails to meet the needs of most young women (Etzkowitz, Kemelgor, Neuschatz, Uzzi and Alonzo 1994). So there are problems about whom one should include in the critical mass; perhaps it can only be more radical women.

Maybe a critical mass should be thought of as a necessary rather than a sufficient condition; maybe we cannot be sure that adding more women will definitely mean changes at the liberal and radical levels. But we can be sure that unless we do add more women, further changes will not be made. Liberal and radical changes are contingent on there being more women involved.

For more women to *use* technology is not sufficient; to do this they only need a superficial knowledge of how the equipment functions. Having significant numbers of women *repairing* equipment, on the other hand, is important because it acknowledges that women can have more than this superficial knowledge – that they can 'get inside' the equipment and understand how it works just as well as men. Just consider what having lots of women car drivers (and not a few female lorry and bus drivers) has done to change the image of women with respect to automobile technology – precisely nothing. But equal numbers of women and men patrolling for motoring organisations such as the Automobile Association and Royal Automobile Club would be much more to the point. Imagine the effect of reversing the stereotypical scenario and a knowledgeable female car mechanic turning up to rescue the stranded, fretting, incompetent male motorist.

It is interesting to speculate about what would happen to women's image if this scenario were to be realized. Men identify with and are possessive towards technology. Their association with it – and women's disassociation from it – is a deeply essential component of their self-image, particularly evident in their relationship with such things as cars. So if this scenario were to come about, men would be faced with a very painful dilemma. *Either* they would have to admit that they do not have the monopoly of something valuable, a monopoly from which they derive so much of their self-image; *or* they could refuse to concede that this ground is valuable by a sexist skill evaluation move, thus downgrading the whole activity. By doing that they would deny women this valuable ground, but only at the expense of depriving themselves of it too. Whichever horn of the dilemma they embrace they would have an identity crisis.

What happens on the domestic scene echoes what happens elsewhere. All the plumbers, electricians, engineers and so on who come to our homes to repair our equipment are men. Further, as Cynthia Cockburn points out, if outsiders don't mend equipment it is usually the men within the household who do it, not the women (Cockburn 1985, Chap 7). It is extremely difficult to see why more women are not involved in these repairs unless such a change represents men having to give up too much of their control of machinery to women, control which, as we have seen, is essential to their self-image.

We have already said that women are half the problem. Complementing men's demand to retain control of technology is women's need to please them by leaving them in control. It is true that women are brought up to regard scientific and technological areas as appropriate to men's talents rather than their own and naturally they want to do jobs for which they believe they are most suited. But job-gendering and gender-channelling run so deep that women's complicity goes beyond 'doing what they do best'; without realizing it, for the most part, 'doing what they do best' means pleasing men by respecting male territory and confining themselves to the jobs men want them to do. The few who do enter the world of computing and stay in it are careful to conform and many are loathe to excel. Those who have the ability and willingness to excel find endless minor obstacles in their way tripping them up at every turn; not one of these obstacles, of course, ever has anything to do with sexism. Perish the thought!

## 10.2   And so to Computing

Large scale changes in computing are likely to happen only in conjunction with large scale changes elsewhere. However, it would be nice to think that, given the immense significance of the information revolution, computing could not only be up with the rest but also helping to lead it.

### Personnel in the Industry

#### Adding More Women Computer Technicians

We have just noted that the large numbers of women drivers, even of lorries and buses, has made little or no difference to their image in relation to automobile technology. Parallel to this, the large number of women using computers in an unsophisticated way, for instance inputting data, has made little difference to the fact that computing is a masculine world just as much as is the world of cars and lorries.

So, what would happen if we were to inject more women into technicians' posts? The men would again be stuck on the horns of a dilemma about their identity – essentially the same dilemma and the same horns that we identified for them about cars.

#### Adding More Women Programmers and Software Designers

We have already seen how, as you move from the central point that the hardware represents, the proportion of women increases: there are more women amongst programmers, analysts and software designers than there are amongst computer engineers and technicians. What would be the effect of adding even more and raising their representation from their present level to nearer 50%, or even greater?

Unlike the scenario where the number of female technicians is increased, it is not difficult to envisage more women being put in charge of teams of programmers, of projects and of departments of all sizes. But again the same argument applies: there will be no change in the dominant ideology in the workplace if the proportion of women at the managerial level is increased and everything else remains the same, that is, if we simply add-more-women.

### Tokenism at the Top

There are some women, but only a very few, at the top in the computing world. So far they have survived. However, the power that men still have at the very top is substantial; there is much to protect. Indeed, I find it interesting how when women attain top posts amidst some publicity (I am thinking here of some prominent public posts both in the UK and overseas, as well as appointments closer to home, but all of them outside computing or technology) they are apparently welcomed. And yet after a period I hear of criticisms – the validity of which it is extremely difficult to judge. *Prima facie* these criticisms are valid and yet one is left with a suspicion that even minor problems are exaggerated by colleagues in the case of these senior women in a way that would not occur if they were men. This is one way in which men keep their power. Whatever the rights and wrongs of these situations, the fact that a woman 'fails' in the job seems to encourage everyone, men and women of all political persuasions, to induce that if one woman cannot do the job, no woman can do it. How long will it be, I wonder, before the British Conservative party allows itself another woman leader, or indeed the Labour party votes for its first woman leader?

Indeed allowing a favoured few women to reach the very top seems to be an attempt to set up 'Aunt Sallys' who, by their very position, are exposed to a great deal of publicity when they are criticised. They therefore act as a conspicuous warning to other women not to get above themselves. Adding these women, far from changing the current climate, reinforces it. Thus, by letting these unfortunate women have brief tenure of these all-important posts, men retain their present power.

### And in Education

Similarly, more women lecturers in higher education and teachers in schools teaching the same topics as are taught now and in the same way means a change – a necessary change, but only a cosmetic one.

My experience is that, in the academic world of computing, men by and large address the men in their audience; the women are invisible. So few women speak in public in this discipline that it is difficult to make the contrary claim about women. But it must be the case that, when more women are present in the audience, they will become less invisible and, just as importantly, women speakers will surely address the women in their audience as much as they address the men. Female speakers will certainly be more conscious of the presence of other women.

## 10.3 How do We Add More Women to Computing?

If adding more women is simply a matter of getting more women to study the subject at school and in higher education and to enter the profession, it is fairly obvious where changes need to be made. Although there is always some resistance to such changes, this is not insurmountable. For instance, the entries in university prospectuses are the first point of contact for prospective students. Given the presumption against women taking up the subject, they need some persuading; and yet the resistance to extending an explicit welcome to women students can be quite astonishing. Nevertheless, under pressure, some of the diehards can be persuaded to include a statement saying, in effect, 'women are welcome'.

## Names and Labels Revisited

What can be done about the names and labels, such as 'science' and 'engineering', which I suggested, do deter women and girls? As I argued in Chapter 7, there really is no logically compelling reason for attaching these names and labels to computing. And, since they put women off, there is good reason not to. Substitutes are not easy to find, but I suggest that the present names and labels are amongst the things that have to be changed before more women can be attracted on a sufficiently large scale. 'Information structuring', 'data organisation', 'data manipulation', 'information retrieval' – many of these are already used for small scale activities; why can't they be used as well to describe large scale activities?

## Examples and Language in Teaching Again

I can see three things that need doing here.

The first is that more examples be introduced based on experiences which, in our present society, are almost exclusively female – embroidery, planning a working day for a parent looking after small children, sorting the washing, dressmaking – would help redress the imbalance. Why not talk of workboxes, or even sewing baskets, as much as toolkits? The reactions of the female hoverfly to the advancing predatory male wouldn't come amiss either![1]

Secondly, and in case what I have just suggested looks like an endorsement of the genderised *status quo*, a parallel development should be that talk of cars and cricket be degenderised, so that women feel at home with them. Conversely, men should be able to talk freely about degenderised 'feminine' activities like embroidery.

Thirdly, gender-neutral subjects should be made more lively than the mathematical examples and sorting employee records that I mentioned in Chapter 7. It's not obvious how this can be achieved but surely, travel, music, gardening, ecology and some sports like tennis and canoeing have a place here.

A few teachers have become more scrupulous in the use of gender-free language; but many still need to recognise that 'he' does not subsume 'she', and that to use it as if it did is a solecism that is simply unacceptable. There are, also, still some who start by using 'he or she' or 'they' but soon lapse into using 'he', apparently not wishing to be seen to be too much at pains to be 'politically correct'. If people

---

[1] There are words and images that I would like to use more often but hesitate to do so. One such word is 'birth'. I did use it once in reference to a new course, but not before I had hesitated and thought carefully, more carefully than I would have thought about many other words; it wasn't its appropriateness I was wondering about – of that I was quite confident – but its impact on the (male) recipient of the letter in which it appeared.

conformed to gender-free requirements, even in cases where their actions belied their words, it would nonetheless make the subject less alien to girls and women.

## Jargon

A further reform of language would be the freeing of computing from jargon that acts as a barrier to newcomers. Most disciplines have jargon – law and medicine are two prime examples. One defence of the use of jargon is that it speeds up communication, but of course only between those who understand the meaning of the words. This defence is justified. Using a single word or label to define a concept or process assists speakers and their listeners in identifying patterns of behaviour or concepts which previously were real experiences and yet woolly and ill-defined. Examples of these words or phrases are 'sexism', 'racism', 'sexual harassment', 'date rape', 'sexist skill evaluation' and some I have introduced here: 'job-gendering' and 'gender-channelling' – all these are jargon words.

So, if jargon does have its uses, why should we complain about it in the computing environment? Jargon and the use of initials in place of the full technical terms have always been, even in the early days, particularly prevalent in speech and literature in the computing community. They serve here, as elsewhere, to create a mystique, to emphasise status; this language is something which only the initiated can expect to understand, the rest are excluded. (Prime examples of this are the use by doctors, until recently, of Latin in prescriptions and present day legalese.) Computing jargon is, in itself, not gender-biased and tends to exclude outsiders regardless of their gender. But since the establishment and the initiated are almost all men, the territory protected by the use of jargon tends to be seen as a male preserve and thus has the effect of disproportionately excluding women. To reduce the use of jargon would make the territory more accessible and this would attract many newcomers and, most importantly, proportionately more women to whom it was previously closed.

## Pictures and Images

The pin-ups and pictures of naked women are no longer present in most of our departments, although they are still sometimes to be seen in places where only men work. But it is surprising how you can still see around the department drawings, sketches and cartoons that illustrate men's superiority and sexual dominance and women's corresponding subordination. I have seen in computing workplaces pictures of sexy but fully clad women – their sexuality is in no way masked by their clothes, their stance and youth say enough. So there are still pictures of women as pin-ups.

The image of the seductive woman is still used to tempt *men* to buy computers: 'The picture shows a woman, naked but for a pair of glasses, tights and high-heeled shoes, sitting cross-legged on an office chair with just a laptop computer to keep her decent. The caption reads 'Wouldn't you just love one on your lap?'(PC Format 1993) Advertisers and manufacturers apologise when complaints are made about these

We encourage our women to wear short skirts or full skirts given the excessive no of hurdles they have to get over.

(deliberate?) errors of judgement, but one is left with the strong impression that these apologies are often feints and that there is no deep-rooted desire to end the practice of using female sex symbols to sell these goods.[2]

Pictures really do convey strong messages. As I write a colleague has on his wall a cartoon showing two men seated at a table being served by a woman dressed as a bunny girl, whilst elsewhere in the department a poster portraying only men advertises a reputable conference on Computer Integrated Manufacturing.

The problem with pictures and language is that we have used both for so long to assert male superiority that it is difficult to disentangle what is sexist from what is not.

Every picture, every advertisement, every computer game has to be judged on its own merits and in the context in which it is being used. It is sometimes helpful to apply tests: 'What if I replaced this naked woman with a naked man? Even if this encouraged women to buy the product, is this an acceptable thing to do?' or 'What if that statement, which sounded a bit suspect to me, had been said about black people rather than women? Wouldn't I be embarrassed if I heard that said about black people?'

We need to take a fresh and sustained look at both pictures and language to ensure that women are portrayed as the 'subject', the one that is doing, rather than as the 'object', the one that is acted on. This would surely help women, at least in a small way, to feel that they might have a place in the profession and to come forward and engage in it.

## Computer Games

I have already discussed the influence of computer games on attitudes to computers. But here I am asking: What if we changed them? Again, an obvious change is simply to introduce more female characters, characters which do not present woman in her stereotypical role. But the introduction of women as central characters to the violent 'beat-'em-up-shoot-'em-up' type of game is an example of adding more women and nicely illustrates the limitations of this first feminist solution. These lithe and

---

[2] And here are two more examples quoted in the Guardian newspaper. In the first, a magazine put out by a software house showed a photo of the seat of a woman's jeans, with a rolled-up copy of the magazine in the pocket headlined 'She's gotta have it'. The same thing happens in prose. In the second example quoted, an advertisement for a laser printer declared that 'She's fast 'n' friendly, amazingly cheap, small, and easily led' (*The Guardian Weekend* 16 April 1994, p60).

strong figures may well be female and dressed in female clothes: leotards, tights and (improbably) high-heeled shoes, but they are simply females pasted onto the male world of these games – the world of the games with all its regrettable aspects (not least the aggression involved) has not changed. Indeed involving more women means, yet again, more women compromising themselves, nicely personified as female Rambos.

There is a blurred hierarchy of acceptability regarding adding more women into computer games. Female Rambo games come at the bottom of this hierarchy. Enter next so-called platform games, e.g. Mickey Mouse, Aladdin and Popeye – these are slightly higher up the hierarchy in that they do not revel in raw violence or aggression. But they still involve a masculine central character with female 'hangers-on'. *Populous* (control of populations) and *Sim City* (town planning) are both examples of what are currently known as 'God games', where the player acts as God; *Tetris* (playing with shapes) and *Lemmings* (preventing lemmings from killing themselves) and card games come next. These do not involve aggression, nor do they involve a central male character and they can be compared with tennis in that they are played both by women and men. Flight simulation games might seem to belong in this category. But in fact they don't since, firstly, they involve the overwhelmingly male activities of piloting planes and, secondly, in spite of what their name implies, they generally involve the aggressive act of shooting down other planes.

Games based on specifically 'female' activities belong to the next level in this hierarchy. One example of this was *Barbie Goes Shopping* – I talk of one example, indeed this is the only one I have been able to identify. And that single instance has long since disappeared. One might indeed dispute whether this game should be so high in the hierarchy, since it reinforces the idea of activities perceived as boring being carried out by the quintessential female. Beyond that, and the top level in this hierarchy, are games involving not just the activities typically associated with women and girls, but activities that represent a world defined by women and for women in which, maybe, we could make all types of shopping exciting for everybody.

## Women's Writing

I stated in Chapter 6 how few computing books have been written by women – indeed, looking down the lists of all the books I have put on reading lists for students, only two have been written by women (Oxborrow 1989, Loomis 1987). Like computer games, this form of communication can be used to illustrate what I mean by add-more-women and here too we can establish a hierarchy of mini-solutions within this first level of criticism.

At the first and bottom layer of this hierarchy we have the situation where more women write in the traditional vein using traditional language and repeating the old examples. It is some sort of solution in that as a result, not only will there be more books by women, but readers will see that women can get involved and, if you like, reproduce this male discourse. But it is still the same male discourse. At the next layer up in the hierarchy we have books written by women which are neutral in their approach to the things that put women off; on the one hand they avoid things that deter women but, on the other, they do not include things designed explicitly to attract them. This can be compared with the layer of computer games that are gender-neutral – card games, etc. (I can't think of a layer corresponding to the Mickey Mouse layer. Perhaps you can think of one.)

Women authors being more explicit in their appeal to women and introducing the 'feminine' into their writing (for instance, in the form of examples more relevant to women's lives) represents the penultimate layer in this hierarchy. Finally, the top layer involves women writing on their own terms, on subjects they choose and in their own style. At this level, these writings must not only exist, they must be accepted as part of the mainstream, possibly alongside the traditional, literature – the existence and acceptability of both would be the norm.

## 10.4   Adding-More-Women is not Enough

Although the criticisms and solutions I have discussed in this chapter may spill over into the second and third levels of feminist criticism, on the whole they are at the more superficial add-more-women level. Of course, one thing that is achieved by adding more women is that more of the available talent is deployed. It is difficult to imagine the acceleration in the development of computing that would take place if most of the talent belonging to women, and now unavailable simply because it belongs to women, were to be used.

Another important point about 'adding-more-women' is that, in spite of its superficiality, it must nonetheless be implemented if anything more radical is to be achieved. Men are hardly likely to 'emasculate' their own subject by themselves; adding more women is a precondition of this happening.

# 11

# The Liberal Level

*All the selfish propensities, the self-worship, the unjust self-preference, which exist among mankind, have their source and root in, and derive their principal nourishment from, the present constitution of the relation between men and women.* John Stuart Mill 1869 (Mill 1984, p324)

## 11.1 The Liberal and Add-More-Women Levels Distinguished

At the second and middle level of criticism and solution we are not principally concerned with the largely quantitative aims of adding more women to the professions, managerial jobs in industry, commerce, public administration and so on. We are more concerned with qualitative changes to the nature of these activities, to the setting in which they are carried out, to the ends they are designed to achieve and, not least in importance, to who makes decisions about all these matters. It is usually a good thing to add more women to the world as we know it; it would be a better thing to add them to an improving world.

This middle level of feminist criticism of science, technology and computing addresses those problems which arise from these fields being dominated by male ruling groups. Because of this domination by men these subjects as practised are not consistent with what Sandra Harding (1991, p55) calls 'feminist politics'. I use this phrase in a particular way. In my description in Part I of the spectrum of different things one can mean by 'feminism', I opted for 'optimal feminism' . By this definition, women are not merely equal to men in ability but also bring to their work attitudes and motivations which are preferable to those that men bring to their work. For instance, women bring a nurturing, caring sensitivity which men tend not to, and a reluctance to dominate where this is unnecessary and they tend to avoid the unproductive competitiveness that features so highly in men's approach to their work.

To say that these attitudes are preferable is, of course, to make a value judgement and, indeed, I want to do just that. There is nothing wrong with value judgements so long as they don't masquerade as facts – indeed life would be impossible without them. We guide our behaviour in the light of them and my value judgement that women's attitudes are preferable to men's does indeed carry with it a whole range of implications as to what should and shouldn't be done. It is this set of practical commitments that I refer to when I use the term 'feminist politics'. These commitments might include the moral view that these disciplines no longer be used for military dominance of Third World societies or to increase profit for the few; and indeed their shape and objectives should not be determined by male-dominated ruling groups in society. These disciplines should instead be used for peaceful, constructive, egalitarian aims. Taking this view, it can be argued that scientists should take more moral responsibility for what they do, instead of arguing that the knowledge they create is neutral and that it is the politicians who decide what is done with it.

We do not want simply to add-more-women to these activities; we want to ensure that such activities are consistent with feminist politics.

It should be said that by feminist politics, and the feminist values that underlie them, I do not mean the politics and values that most women espouse at present. It is patently obvious that most women do not hold such values. I do not even mean the politics and values espoused by all those who call themselves feminists, whether men or women. I mean a set of values that I myself hold and wish to commend and which I am still struggling to formulate; a set of values that overlaps to a considerable extent with those already held by many feminists. And, of course, this set of values is derived from what I have asserted to be a preferable approach to work – an approach that is strongly associated with women rather than men.

The opportunity to bring these new values into the workplace arises from women being introduced fresh to positions of power and able therefore to question the presuppositions and ideas of those already familiar with these positions of power. Much of the opportunity to change things comes about because women are new to the situation; we are not relying on them being better people, they are fresh people, bringing with them the preferable set of attitudes that I have been discussing. Similarly we are not condemning men as devils; they are merely imbued with old and superseded values. Insofar as I am not claiming that women are angels about to drive out the male devils, I have to admit that the possibility of a golden age is more remote. It is possible that, if change is too slow, women will be infected by present masculine attitudes and change will occur more slowly or cease altogether.

One way in which the set of preferable attitudes that women tend to bring to the workplace can be corrupted may be seen in the way some women compete for and are active in top jobs in the professions. Such women feel they are doing the right thing; there is an aura of moral righteousness about them, that they are not just furthering their own interests but those of womankind as well. And indeed insofar as they are helping to achieve greater equality of opportunity and enabling women to get to the top, they are to a limited extent working for the good of womankind. But the extent to which they are doing this is indeed very limited – a mere quantitative change at the top. Most of these aspiring women working to get to the top use and accept the huge mass of support staff who underpin the organisations constituting the 'world of work'. These aspiring women accept that the low status jobs, those of secretaries, cleaners, housewives and so on, on which the structure of the workplace depends, are held by women. And although they may pay lip service to changing this state of affairs, in practice they do nothing about it. So while these pursuers of equal opportunities look highly moral, what they are doing is tantamount to an endorsement of the *status quo* for the majority of women.

These aspiring women will often argue, of course, that if they are given equal opportunity to rise to the top because they are able, the other side of the coin is that some men are liable to sink to the bottom because they are less able. Given an equal distribution of ability between the genders, the situation would then, in theory, tend towards one of equal proportions of women and men at all levels. But the pressures not to suggest change and innovation come from all quarters. How often have you heard a female personnel officer propose a programme for recruiting more men as secretaries and domestic staff? Even if they wanted to they just don't dare; it's more than their jobs are worth. They and their other female colleagues heartily endorse the idea that all women should not be cleaners, but will do nothing to implement their professed view that not all cleaners should be women.

So these aspiring women are not even aiming to implement add-more-women in a thorough going way by working towards an equal distribution of women and men across the board, including the degendering of support work.[1] If such women do not even argue for real equality of opportunity within the present hierarchies, how far are they from the liberal level attitude of questioning the desirability of hierarchies in their present form?

Take, for instance, the assumption that if equal opportunity produces winners it must also in the nature of things produce losers; that if some women make it to the top because they are able, then some men must sink to the bottom because they are less able. We may wish to retain some form of hierarchy and in some sense there may still have to be winners and losers but this doesn't necessarily point to a situation where 'the winner takes all'. Who wants to return to the days when hierarchies so often involved the key to the executive loo, the right to use the executive canteen or to have a larger desk than the person next door? Instead 'professional' women and men could do more of their own photocopying and typing, make all their own appointments and ensure that decisions are more democratically made.

However, some form of hierarchy may be necessary so that in consequence there are people at the top and people at the bottom. It is difficult to see how one can avoid a person or set of people taking ultimate responsibility for an organisation, but who these people are to be and the responsibilities they are to bear must be democratically decided. These 'organisers' must in turn delegate tasks and those to whom jobs are delegated have responsibilities too. But, as always, with these duties go rights – rights to make decisions and to share in the rewards. Not only do those at the top have to be democratically chosen but more of the decisions hitherto made at

---

[1] We have already seen (Etzkowitz et al. 1994) how women in the academic sphere, and no doubt elsewhere, tend when promoted to adopt a male point of view.

the top should be devolved to the rest of the hierarchy. If these democratic processes take up what has in the past been termed 'valuable research time', so be it; it is an important component of the liberal solution. And once work has been allocated, those responsible should be left to complete it without undue supervision.

Another feature of a hierarchy that might be acceptable at the liberal level would be one where being at the top is not regarded as a reward for individual excellence but a responsibility and an opportunity to work for the common good. Of course, this is already true and both these elements are quite compatible with one another. What is being argued here is that if both these aspects are retained, there should be a considerable shift of emphasis between them – a shift which could produce a quite different climate in which people can work.

## 11.2   Science at the Liberal Level

So far we have considered very general aspects of liberal level values concerning, for instance, the nature of hierarchies in which all workers might find themselves, not just those who work in computing. Let us now focus more on computing by briefly looking at science at the liberal level. As we saw in the previous chapter, the reason for this is that computing is often regarded in the popular mind, and in the university prospectus, as something akin to a science and, moreover, it derives much of its image from the scientific tradition. It may be misguided to think of computing as a science but insofar as people do think of it in this way they will, as we shall see, take to it the attitudes appropriate to scientific work. This particularly affects in a negative way the attitudes of girls and women who might otherwise take up computing. First then, some comments on science in general at the liberal level.

### The Nature of Competition among Scientists

An important shift at the liberal level concerns the aims of individual scientists. Taking a naive view of the present situation, science is an objective pursuit of truth by individual scientists who are themselves objective and have the discovery of truth as their sole aim. But this *is* a naive view of science as it is practised at the moment, and clearly individual scientists are very much motivated by the desire for self-promotion, academic honours (including Nobel prizes and fellowships of learned societies) and, of course, competition for the all-important funding. Each scientist is anxious that it should be his (and occasionally her) hypothesis that is vindicated and takes the honours. Taking this more realistic view, what happens is that the hypotheses of each non-objective scientist are subject to criticism in an arena of public debate; it is in this way that work that is self-interestedly motivated is transmogrified into a body of objective knowledge.

There is a distant parallel here with Adam Smith's view of some 'invisible hand' transmuting the self-interestedly motivated activities of individual entrepreneurs, each bent on maximising his or her own profits, into a system that works for the welfare and benefit of the consumer. Science as it is practised at the moment reflects this 'capitalist' scenario. But just as Marxism offers us an alternative view of what the motivation for production could be, so it offers an alternative view as to what the motivation for science could be. Alienation is a crucial Marxist concept concerned with the fragmentation of our lives and the separation of things that should be united – for example, workers from their work and workers from one another. It is the latter that is relevant here. Capitalism requires us to be competitive at both the institutional and the personal levels. Where there could be a sense of community and a sense of common purpose amongst colleagues there is isolation. It would be highly desirable to have a shift in motivation and the outlook that underpins it towards a more disinterested, less selfish, motivation both in the economy and in the pursuit of scientific activity. Some adjustment towards the 'naive' view of science could, and should, be made and science be pursued by individuals more for the sake of truth. The aim should be not just to make a greater contribution to human welfare but also to the welfare of the planet's ecology.

## Science and Emotion

Another demand of the liberal criticism of science is that there be a full acknowledgement of emotions and feelings. At present, the very language in which scientific papers are couched creates the illusion that scientists don't have feelings and even that experiments are not undertaken by people. 'X was done' rather than 'We did X'. Even in the relative informality of the common room and corridor the talk is of anything other than matters of emotional importance. (This is, of course, true of other male-dominated environments and is not peculiar to science.) The refusal to acknowledge emotions creates an environment in which many women, with their ability and inclination to express emotions, feel alien. Of course, to some extent this potential is muted in women, influenced as they are by masculine *mores*, but the potential is a considerable one for all concerned; men would benefit from following the lead of women in this matter while women are presently disadvantaged by following men's lead. The suppression of emotion is preoccupying, diverting energy away from the development of new ideas; to the extent that people actively suppress emotions, they are too busy to be innovative.

## 11.3   From Science to Technology and Engineering

If the agenda for science can be set by the objectives and priorities of a male-dominated society, how much more so is this true in the case of technology? There is at least some plausibility in talk of 'pure scientific knowledge gathered for its own sake', even if this is largely a myth. One aspect of this myth is that science and scientific research develop along the lines dictated by their own internal logic, relatively uninfluenced by factors external to them. But no one thinks in terms of such myths in the case of technology, which is essentially the application of knowledge to change the world in ways dictated by desires, policies, fashions, etc. which are not part of that knowledge – in other words, to change the world according to the priorities of a society which is dominated by men. Look how technology advances by leaps and bounds in time of war. And remember Star Wars? Officially known as the Strategic Defence Initiative, this was a call for technology to do, not what was dictated by some internal logic to be the next step forward, but what was best to beat the Soviets, even if it was far beyond the current technological capability.

It goes without saying that the factors external to technology which dictate its priorities and programmes should be those of a society dominated by feminist ideals in the sense I have defined them in the first section of this chapter.

## 11.4   Computing at the Liberal Level

### Co-operation in the 'Process' and the 'Product'

The liberal criticism is concerned with both the way in which computer systems are produced and the way in which they are used; or to use Joan Greenbaum's labels the 'process' and the 'product' (Greenbaum 1990).

To bring out what this liberal level criticism involves, let us look at what is all too often the present state of affairs in systems design. Often those people whose work is analysed and redefined are the female clerks, secretaries and library assistants. They are typically allowed little say in either the analytical or the development process. The systems analyst (often male) is called in from an outside department or organisation. Then using traditional systems development methods, he (or perhaps she) asks questions about what tasks the clerks currently perform. He designs and initiates the implementation of a new system and then specifies what they have to do under this new system. The clerks often have little idea of how their work fits into the work of the organisation (hierarchies are to blame for this, but systems methods do nothing to rectify it). Nor is there any provision in the traditional methods which allows the clerks to decide what input they would like to make to the analytical process.

Now imagine the following transformation. Marja Vehviläinen (1991) in a study of clerical workers in Finland persuaded the women she worked with to define what questions they thought were important for the analysis: 'With whom do I work?' 'What do we do together?' Those for whom these questions were not so important were more interested in the tasks they performed and were therefore encouraged to ask questions about those tasks. Another woman was more concerned about her personal well-being: 'Is this work monotonous?' All these different views were encouraged, giving the clerks control over the development process; each one determined for herself which were the most important questions, thus moving away from the traditional 'scientific' systems development methods.

This approach is called participatory or co-operative systems design and development and was pioneered by Enid Mumford in the 1970s ((Mumford and Henshall 1979, Mumford 1983)). A typical example of participatory systems design is the 'City Libraries' study by Eileen Green *et al* (Green, Owen and Pain 1991). Library assistants were encouraged by means of study circles to put forward ideas and articulate their views as part of a programme for the computerisation of a library. Here, however, they went a small step further than Marja Vehvilaïnen did in her study. The library assistants were encouraged, and to some extent succeeded, in setting the criteria for details of implementation. They were concerned about sending out letters requesting the return of overdue books that had already been returned. The system developer was not concerned about the upset readers whom the library assistants had to face, being more concerned with the efficiency of central stamping. When the assistants urged that customer care was more important, the developer was reduced to saying that it would be expensive to keep stocks of good quality paper at each branch; branches might run out of it. Where the professional system developer wanted a centralised, streamlined system, the librarians, more conscious of readers' needs, asked for, and got, more control at branch level.

So here we have the end-users actively involved in the analysis and design process, not only participating in it but determining its direction.

Yet another example of co-operative systems design is described by Ian Sommerville and his colleagues (Sommerville, Rodden, Sawyer, Bentley and Twidale 1992). This study concerns the work of air traffic controllers. The word 'co-operative' is used here to describe different areas of co-operation. It refers first to co-operation between anthropologists and software engineers in the design of the software system for the air traffic controllers, i.e. co-operation in the 'process' of system development. It also involved the co-operation of the air traffic controllers themselves in the study. This is where the anthropologists came in, using their skills to get people to give the necessary information and to give it undistorted.

Interestingly, in these studies much of the work of eliciting the necessary information from end-users was done by sociologists or anthropologists, not by the system developer behaving in the traditional way. Significantly, it is not part of the traditional system developer's expertise to work in this manner – a fact which underlines the extent of the change involved in this new approach.

Co-operation not only occurs in the process of developing a system, it also occurs in the 'product' i.e. in the system itself, the way it is used and the effect it has on people. This is strongly suggested by a name often used for this whole area of activity, namely Computer Supported Co-operative Work or CSCW. The term 'product' includes the interaction among individual workers on the one hand and between groups of workers and computers on the other. The air traffic control study highlights this type of co-operation. Air traffic control is very much team work (teams stay together for years) and is essentially co-operative in nature. Some of the activities involved – for example, moving slips of paper around – make the work very difficult to automate. This is something the traditional computer scientists seemed to accept more readily in this instance than they do in the case of the office-workers. Articulating the complaints of office workers has been left to those researchers who, by and large, do not come from within the office.

There is yet another variation on this theme of co-operation in the 'product', and that is co-operation in simultaneous use of machines. In the early days when we mostly used punched cards or paper tape to input programs and data into the machine there was no possibility of two or more people co-operating in its use at one and the same time. In those years the computers were isolated in a room designed to house them and it might have looked as if there were a pooling of effort on the part of all the people using the same machine. There was nonetheless a one-to-one relationship between the programmer and the machine. Each programmer wrote his or her own program and then sorted out the programming errors (often termed 'bugs'), possibly with help from others; but the responsibility for getting it working rested with the individual. Programmers worked in teams, but each member was given a set of programs or procedures to write and wrote those bits on his or her own. Thus although it appeared that the people were co-operating, because they all used the same machine, they were not.

The mode of operation with which we are now familiar is one where each person sits at a VDU writing programs, or communicating with the machine in some other way. This has arisen at least in part from the historical context. Part of the liberal solution involves the development of different modes of operation. For example, these days one can find two or more people sitting at their own work stations making simultaneous contributions to the current activity. In some ways this is like playing computer games involving more than one person. So in spite of the fact that each person is sitting at his or her own machine and each appears to be doing his or her own thing, in fact they may well be co-operating.

## Ways of Telling

I mentioned in the context of scientific reporting the tendency to use an impersonal style and later I mentioned how computing has inherited much from the scientific tradition. There is still a strong tendency in the academic and business worlds to write in this same impersonal style, in the 'true' scientific manner. Perhaps a partial explanation for this lies in the idea of the repeatability of experiments, that one ought to be able to get the same results independently of the accidents of where, when and by whom they were carried out.

In contrast to this, there is a refreshing tendency nowadays for manuals for popular computer software to be written differently. They are lighter in style and address the reader more directly. Certainly no one is going to engage the attention of school-age children by writing instructions for them in the third person. 'Using Prune 3-2-1 the user can produce graphics of a quality that has never been seen before' doesn't exactly 'grab' the reader; 'With Prune 3-2-1 you can produce drawings of a quality you have never seen before!' does. Turning back to the worlds of business and academia, the impersonality of 'The student must take care that . . .' distances teacher from student. 'You must take care that . . .' involves the author with the reader and the teacher with the student. This style does not represent a relaxation of the relationship between student and teacher – if anything it is more commanding. What is important is that there is a greater degree of involvement between the two. And there is no reason why students should not be encouraged to use the first person and write 'I did X' in their reports.

## Life Stories

Life histories have a role to play in the attainment of the liberal ideal. Alan Turing's 'enigmatic' life has provided material for an absorbing biography (Hodges 1985). Giving more prominence to the lives and experiences of computer scientists would add another dimension to the study of the subject. Learning what application a person was working on and in what industry when they developed an important and well-known data structure, sorting algorithm or piece of hardware provides added interest to an otherwise dull topic. Finding out why that person did it, what buildings he or she worked in, what men and women wore, and reading descriptions of the working environment can add life and texture to a subject, give it more meaning – even sorting algorithms could become humanised! Computing could be seen as an achievement of people, people with hopes, fears, weaknesses, virtues and aspirations.

We need not only rely on carefully written, well-polished biographies. Oral histories can provide a further source of material. Most of us do not consider our working lives worth writing about; we do not expect our stories to be distinguished from those of others. This is especially true of women, who tend to be invisible in their workplace and whose input to a smoothly run department is difficult to measure. Encouraging women in particular to record their own experiences of their working lives would result in histories which would give us a better idea of their part in the dynamics of the workplace. People are now beginning to direct their research towards women and their role (Adam et al. 1994). If people are encouraged to talk about not just their paid work but all the other work they have to do and the impact on their mobility of such factors as childbearing, childrearing and living with a partner and their motivations for career moves, then they may be persuaded to tell things they might not otherwise. Simply relating ideas already thought through is just one aspect of this. Under questioning from a sympathetic interviewer over a period of hours, an interviewee can look much more deeply into her history and through a variety of trigger mechanisms can recall forgotten events from the distant past. She can then examine with the advantage of the passage of time and the resulting dulling of emotion her own motivations for taking a job, embarking on a project or choosing to have a baby. Reading women's life histories is something really quite novel and such histories provide a new slant on the way in which computing as a career has developed.

## 11.5   Acknowledging People

If there is one theme running through this discussion of the liberal level it is that people are important and should be acknowledged as such. In the examples of co-operative, or participatory, design I considered the possibility of individuals other than the computing 'experts' having a say in the design and daily running of new systems. I suggested the re-evaluation and softening of hierarchies. I advocated allowing feelings and emotions into the workplace and making reporting less impersonal. I also recommended giving attention to biographies and life histories.

In all this is a recognition of the fact that computing is a human activity carried out by people who matter, not just the twentieth-century space-age equivalent of the 'hand' in the Victorian mill. In both cases it is wrong to treat people merely as adjuncts to a machine and a system. The aim is to add women to work situations in which people are regarded as important and multi-dimensional.

# 12

# The Radical Level

*The most important thing women have to do is to stir up the zeal of women themselves. We have to stimulate their aspirations – to bid them not despair of anything, nor think anything beyond their reach, but try their faculties against all difficulties.* John Stuart Mill 1869 (Mill 1910, p209)

## 12.1  The Gendering of Science

The second or liberal level of criticism and solution does at least recognise that it is not good enough simply to involve more women in science as it is currently practised, not good enough simply to add-more-women. But even this liberal solution fails to recognise and react to the essentially masculine nature of science. What do I mean by 'the essentially masculine nature of science'? I do not mean that science *has* to be masculine but that it happens to have been imbued with this masculine character as a result of the combined action of those two familiar phenomena, job-gendering and gender-channelling. Indeed, it would be hard to think of many better examples of the combined effect of these two factors than science, engineering and technology. As I have already observed, girls are not generally brought up to think that sciences like physics, electronics and engineering of various sorts are appropriate activities for them. At the same time these activities themselves are presented as predominantly fitted for men to pursue.

My point is that, while this happens, relations between women and science are affected at each of my three levels. Women obviously are grossly under-represented in the sciences, giving rise to the need to add more women. Secondly, at the liberal level, men dominate these activities, deciding how they are to take place, who gets official sanction for their projects in terms of both funding and honours. Men also are the ones who decide how scientific knowledge is to be used. The liberal level solution does at least recognise that these features need to be put right. But it falls short by failing to recognise that science has been deeply imbued with masculinity which, of course, accounts for the dearth of women – they feel it is just not their territory. This masculine character also underpins the liberal level faults and yet goes beyond both these two relatively superficial levels into the underlying ethos of these disciplines.

This can be seen, for instance, in Carolyn Merchant's examination of the Baconian ideas in the development of western science (Merchant 1980); other feminist writers have agreed on and reiterated the strength of this influence (Jordanova 1980, Wajcman 1991). In its most extreme form Bacon's portrayal of the discovery of nature's secrets was expressed in metaphors of rape. One very explicit example of this has already been quoted in Chapter 7:

> For you have but to follow and as it were hound nature in her wanderings, and you will be able when you like to lead and drive her afterward to the same place again . . . Neither ought a man to make scruple of entering and penetrating into these holes and corners when the inquisition of truth is his whole object.

Here is an analogy with the torture chamber:

> For like as a man's disposition is never well known or proved till he be crossed, nor Proteus ever changed shapes till he was straitened and held fast, so nature exhibits herself more clearly under the trials and vexations of art [mechanical devices] than when left to herself.

Another analogy is with women's reproductive function:

> There is therefore much ground for hoping that there are still laid up in the womb of nature many secrets of excellent use having no affinity or parallelism with anything that is now known . . . only by the method which we are now treating can they be speedily and suddenly and simultaneously presented and anticipated.

And, finally, nature in bondage:

> . . . she is put in constraint, molded, and made as it were new by art and the hand of man; as in things artificial.

(Bacon (1870) quoted by Carolyn Merchant (1980, pp 168, 169, 170))

## Boycott-Science

The metaphors here may be specific to Bacon and particular historical periods,[1] but the scientific enterprise of which these metaphors are symptomatic is a general one: a despoilment of nature as unscrupulous and brutal as is necessary to get the required results, a project essentially masculine in its conception. The radical criticism is that since science is based on so masculine an ideology, it can never accommodate women and, should they get involved, they lose their identity as women. In the face of this criticism two possible solutions present themselves. The first is that women should have nothing to do with science and should eschew it. This solution I identify as *boycott-science* (the opposite of add-more-women).

[1] Though don't forget my fully contemporary forceps-wielding colleague of Chapter 7!

### Find-A-New-Science

It can be argued, however, that it would be disastrous for women if they kept out of science; 'we live in a scientific culture; to be scientifically illiterate is simply to be illiterate – a condition of far too many women and men already' (Harding 1991, p55). This quotation implies an alternative radical solution: science should not be scrapped nor should women deprive themselves of it but it should be transformed in such a way that women can enter it without any loss of identity or integrity. In other words, the masculine character of science, exacerbated by in-depth gender-channelling and job-gendering, should be removed.

Indeed it could be argued that my optimal feminism implies that this masculine character should be replaced by a feminine one. Instead of 'a despoilment of nature as unscrupulous and brutal as is necessary', a project I have identified as essentially masculine, the approach to science would be one characterised by Barbara McClintock as 'letting the material speak to you', being prepared to 'let the material tell you what to do' (Keller 1983). What could be called an intuitive empathy might replace the ruthlessness of the masculine approach. I use the phrase *find-a-new-science* to identify this second radical solution.

## 12.2   From Science to Technology and Engineering

Science can at least be represented as an attempt to understand the world sympathetically. But this characterisation is much less plausible in the case of technology, which appears to be even more blatantly masculinised, a project to make nature do what we want 'her' to do, the spirit of which is amply illustrated in the quotations from Bacon already cited.

But just how masculine is technology? Here there are two views that are crucially different. The first and more radical view is that technology is so essentially masculine that no change can really demasculinise it. It is not simply that men dominate technology by their sheer numbers, not simply that they control its agenda and objectives, nor even that they use technology in order to control other people, especially women. In this extreme radical view, technology *is* control *simpliciter*. And that is why it is essentially a masculine project.

For example, engineering as a technology implies intervention and control; we speak of 'engineering a situation'. In sociology the term 'social engineering' is used to describe the practice of intervening in people's lives to change them in some way. Similarly, 'genetic engineering' is used to describe human intervention in the process of the development of genes. So, the notion of engineering is redolent of a long-standing interventionist approach in science and technology – an approach that is essentially masculine and could never be anything else. This view leads to the more radical alternative *boycott-technology*.

The second and milder of these radical views of technology is that it is not inherently a masculine project but that it has been hijacked by men in order, amongst other things, to control women and enhance the feeling of solidarity amongst the dominant males. One exponent of this view is Judy Wajcman, who argues that men arrange affairs so that:

> Men's affinity with technology is ... seen as integral to the constitution of male gender identity. 'Technology enters into our sexual identity; femininity is incompatible with technological competence; to feel technically competent is to feel manly (Cockburn 1985, p12).'
> (Wajcman 1991, p38)

From this perspective, although 'gender construction is an ongoing ideological and cultural process with a long history', that history can be brought to an end. There is no reason why a future technical culture has to be like the present one which 'expresses and consolidates relations amongst men' (Wajcman 1991, p38). Placed in a different ideological and cultural setting, technology could be demasculinised. We cannot afford to be totally radical in the short run and to scrap existing technology – after all that would mean throwing the non-stick frying-pan out with the bath water. But, in the first instance, we need to use existing technology in different ways, in ways which feminists and their sympathisers can choose. This view is tantamount to *find-a-new-technology*. In other words, freed from gender bias technology is something women could enter into without compromise.

Perhaps the first step in find-a-new-technology is that women must be able to establish their fair share of control across the board, in all spheres of activity. Indeed optimal feminism suggests that they should perhaps have rather more control than the men – at least temporarily. For example, in the home control of technology should be such that the time spent on housework will be reduced by at least 50%. Housework certainly isn't the whole story; there is health care too. Take, for example, the technology of birth control. The female contraceptive pill, while clearly a boon to many, was in the 1960s foisted on others who had serious misgivings about side-effects. But neither then nor now did anyone speak seriously about the development and widespread availability of a male contraceptive pill. In some relationships it might work very well and yet it has never been an option. Technology should not be used by one half of the population to control the other; it should serve everybody and allow all to have control over their own health, work and leisure activities.

The changes I have just outlined are merely at the liberal level. They might be, however, sufficiently comprehensive and far-reaching to lead to radical changes which we cannot at present predict. Perhaps the metaphor of the leopard and its spots could be recruited here. At the liberal level the leopard would merely have to change its habitat and diet. At the radical level, however, the leopard would have to change its spots. What I have just described are massive alterations to the leopard's habitat and diet which might lead to changes in its spots – changes which I cannot yet envisage.

## 12.3 Boycott-Science and Computing

I have already noted how disastrous it would be to exclude women entirely from scientific endeavour. This would be just as true of keeping women out of the information revolution, the huge potential of which is only just beginning to be seen and of which neither the magnitude nor most of the components can be predicted. By the very logic of the situation it is impossible to be specific about fundamentally new developments and Kuhnian revolutions. Kuhn's view of the development of science is, very briefly, that a scientific community accepts a single paradigm made up of the general theoretical assumptions and laws that it uses to explain and predict phenomena. While the paradigm is able to do this job, the scientific community will continue to work within it, doing what Kuhn calls 'normal science'. After a while, however, the difficulties in explaining phenomena in terms of the paradigm become greater and greater and a crisis state develops. This is resolved by the rejection of the old paradigm and the emergence of an entirely new one, which increasingly attracts the allegiance of the scientific community. This is what Kuhn calls a scientific revolution, which of course introduces a new phase of 'normal science' and which will itself in turn eventually be subject to a crisis and further revolution and so on.[2]

One can be quite sure that the information revolution will be a major factor, if not *the* major factor, shaping the future. Therefore, for women to exclude themselves would be to deny themselves any chance of an equal intellectual standing with men. And, as we shall see in the next section, there are developments possible within computing which will enable women to enter it without compromising their identity.

## 12.4 Find-A-New-Science and Computing

### The Potential Influence of Sherry Turkle

How, then, is computing to be made inherently more feminist? Sherry Turkle, both in her book *The Second Self* (Turkle 1984a) and in a later article (Turkle and Papert 1990), develops ideas which suggest a radical solution. In both these works the emphasis is not on what is achieved in computing nor the applications for which software is used. The focus is on people's attitude to computers and on how the software is written and the approach programmers take.

In her earlier writings Turkle (1984a) and (Turkle 1984b) describes the ways in which different groups react to and make use of computers. She describes the reactions of children, adolescents, computer hobbyists, hackers and academics. Rather than seeing the computer (and its software) simply as a 'tool' which is used to achieve a pre-determined objective, she examines the reactions of the users and the way in which they use computers to reflect some of their own personal traits and to help them acquire skills which were not apparent previously. She describes their reactions to computers:

[2]For a short and readable description of Kuhn's paradigms see A F Chalmers (1978, Chapter 8).

Most considerations of the computer describe it as rational, uniform, constrained by logic. I look at the computer in a different light, not in terms of its nature as an 'analytical engine', but in terms of its 'second nature' as an evocative object, an object that fascinates, disturbs equanimity, and precipitates thought (p3).

In these earlier writings Turkle discusses programming techniques she labels as 'hard' and 'soft' mastery. She describes some of the children (of either sex) she observed and interviewed as being either hard or soft masters. Both types achieve their objective (in one example this is drawing a space craft) but the one by hard mastery, 'the imposition of will over the machine', and the other by soft mastery, 'the mastery of the artist: try this, wait for a response, try something else, let the overall shape emerge from an interaction with the medium' (pp102–3). Although Turkle describes some boys as being soft masters, she subsequently writes that 'girls tend to be soft masters, while the hard masters are overwhelmingly male'. Soft mastery is reminiscent of the intuitive empathy expressed by Barbara McClintock when she spoke of 'letting the material speak to you' (which I mentioned as part of the discussion on the radical criticism of science).

As part of the hard mastery approach Turkle identifies the 'divide-and-conquer' strategy. Hard masters break a problem into manageable parts and solve the parts before bringing the whole together. Soft masters, on the other hand, do not get involved in advance planning but solve the problem by 'negotiation and experimentation with the machine' (again, contrast this sensitive approach with the brutal despoilment inherent in the Baconian tradition and echoed in 'hard mastery').

In a later paper entitled *Epistemological Pluralism*, Turkle and her co-author, Papert, identify two distinct approaches to programming style – the formal and the concrete – which can be seen as a development of the earlier distinction between hard and soft mastery. The formal or canonical approach is the traditional structured 'divide-and-conquer' technique commonly taught, certainly at the tertiary level. The concrete approach is one in which the programmers perfect small pieces of program and then build something larger out of these small components. They 'feel their way' from one component to another. Those to whom this style of programming appeals tend to shun prepackaged procedures; they dislike the opacity of the black boxes which these libraries of procedures represent, wanting to have a feel for all the components of their work.

The concrete approach also involves the creation of objects, quite complex objects, to which the programmer can get close. Turkle and Papert cite children using the Logo icons the turtle and sprite to create objects with which they have empathy. The popularity of icons in other more sophisticated systems may foreshadow the development of a new concrete style involving the use of screen objects.[3]

---

[3] The apparent popularity of object-oriented programming techniques and the use of object-oriented languages and systems would suggest a surge of interest in a concrete style of programming. In fact, I doubt whether these systems are as well liked as their frequency of use suggests. My (admittedly anecdotal) experience is that while the concept of an object is easy enough to grasp, the way in which these objects are defined and used makes it quite difficult for both the newcomer and the old-hand to use them fluently. And

Like soft mastery, the concrete approach is reminiscent of Barbara McClintock's relationship to the chromosomes on which, or rather with which, she worked: 'when I was really working with them I wasn't outside, I was down there. I was part of the system' (Keller 1983, p141).

The popularity of icons suggests that only a 'weak' form of pluralism is likely to develop – that is one in which, although people have a choice, they all tend to adopt the same style. The radical solution requires a 'strong' pluralism – one in which several styles are followed. Which style is employed is a matter of choice; people are free to demasculinise their style if they wish. Finishing the product is not the only goal; doing it the way you want is another.

Turkle and Papert suggest that, as part of the development of the concrete approach, logic would be an essential ingredient of computing but would not dominate – it would be 'on tap not on top' (Turkle and Papert 1990, p133). Beyond the fact that we shall still need formal logic and mathematics, it is impossible to say what will happen.

## Artificial Intelligence and the Radical Level

A long-cherished dream of recent science fiction has been the development of highly intelligent, rational thinking-machines programmed to operate on vast databanks of knowledge according to strict laws of logic, uninfluenced by emotional factors. These computers would simulate the human mind, indeed produce a super version of human intelligence – super, in fact, in two ways. The first is that they would have the whole of contemporary human knowledge at their disposal, something which an individual human being cannot have; secondly, they would be super in that they would operate solely along purely logical lines, undistorted by extraneous influences.

This, in a not very much less dramatic form, has been the object of an important branch of computing known as artificial intelligence (AI). As its name implies, the aim is to program computers to think intelligently. The presupposition of the main version of AI is that intelligence involves the manipulation of symbols and propositions (for example, statements such as 'Water freezes at 0°C' and 'The earth revolves around the sun'). It would do this according to fixed rules of logic and analogical inference. The power of such machines to solve problems by applying existing knowledge to particular situations will be, it is thought, enormous.

The first steps towards the creation of this power have been taken in what is called 'knowledge engineering', the name given to those sections of AI that concern the creation of 'expert' or 'knowledge-based systems'. An example of expert systems was briefly mentioned in Chapter 3, the knowledge of medical experts being built into computer programs to facilitate diagnoses. One of the most ambitious schemes of this sort is Cyc, a ten year project due to close before the end of the 1990s and paid for by American industry, which it is intended will incorporate most of contemporary US consensual or common-sense knowledge. By common-sense

---

some of these languages, like C++ and Smalltalk, are old concepts dressed up in new guises – we are often told an integer variable can be perceived as an object.

knowledge is meant, for example, background knowledge like 'Your nose is part of your face' and basic facts like 'Edinburgh is the capital of Scotland' (Elkan and Greiner 1993, Lenat and Guha 1989).

Although AI met with some early and promising successes, it has since been subjected to a barrage of criticism which severely called into question its claim to be able to encapsulate the whole of human thinking and knowledge. One of its presuppositions, as we have seen, is that the units of thinking are propositions expressed in linguistic symbols – in plain English, collections of words. But is this really the case? Babies and small children know people and know facts about people and things before they can talk.

Again, much of our knowledge is not 'knowing *that*' but 'knowing *how*'.

> You probably know how to ride a bicycle. Does that mean you can formulate specific rules that would successfully teach someone else how to do it? How would you explain the difference between the feeling of falling over and the perfectly normal sense of being slightly off balance when turning? . . . You can ride a bicycle because you possess something called 'know-how', which you acquired from practice and sometimes painful experience. The fact that you can't put what you have learned into words means that know-how is not accessible to you in the form of facts and rules. If it were, we would say that you 'know that' certain rules produce proficient bicycle riding (Dreyfus and Dreyfus 1986, p16).

This amounts to a claim that AI cannot incorporate 'knowing how'. Another criticism is based on the problem of deciding who the experts are, whose 'expert knowledge' is to be built into expert systems. That some beliefs constitute true knowledge may be uncontroversial, but who is to decide that astrology is mere belief and not knowledge or that capitalist economic analysis is superior to its Marxist rival? Given the Christian claim that there is only one god and the Hindu claim that there are many, who decides which of these is belief and which, if either, is knowledge?

Certain diagnostic manuals of mental illness such as DSM-III-R[4] (used very widely in the US) contain, as Irene Stiver (1991) points out, criteria covertly biased against women. If these criteria, and other similarly biased criteria, are incorporated into expert systems then this will make the expert systems themselves biased against women. Furthermore enshrining them in expert systems is likely to give these biased criteria even more influence. Similar considerations might be given to the encapsulation in legal expert systems of laws biased against women, for example, the law that defines what counts as premeditated murder of a violent husband by his wife.

These kinds of criticism have often led to AI being considered to be intrinsically anti-feminine. Insofar as women's thinking is deemed to be more intuitive, and therefore 'less logical', than that of men, it is men's thinking that is given the endorsement of being included in AI projects and women's thinking that is

---

[4] The Diagnostic and Statistical Manual of Mental Disorders, the American Psychiatric Association's official classification system.

denigrated by its exclusion. Moreover women's skills often involve 'knowing how' rather than 'knowing that', and these are similarly excluded.

These exclusions, together with the problem of deciding whose knowledge is to be counted as expert, lead Alison Adam, for example, to argue that AI favours the 'knowledge' and thinking of orthodox, white, middle-class western males (Adam 1994).

> Many women's skills for instance about midwifery and childrearing, herbal medicine and the like, do not take on the status of knowledge.

It seems to me that the extent to which AI tilts the playing field against women's skills and ways of thinking can be exaggerated. Men also have non-propositional skills, knowledge which involves 'knowing how' rather than 'knowing that'.

As we have seen in Chapter 9, men also use intuition (a further way of thinking over and above 'knowing how', in spite of Dreyfus and Dreyfus equating the two). Intuition cannot be included in AI because it does not work according to rules. But although an important way of thinking for men is thereby excluded, it is women who have developed intuition as a skill *par excellence*, particularly at the interpersonal level. So although both genders lose out by intuition not being included, women lose out more than men.

The purpose of this discussion of AI is to provide an example of the need to look at science at the radical level, particularly at computing, and to identify any inherent features that might compromise the identities of women entering it. The challenge then is to see whether we can find-a-new-science, a radically alternative version which avoids this distortion of women's identity. That the dominance of propositional AI compromises men too, albeit not quite to the same extent, does not alter the fact that women entering it are compromised. And behind this compromise affecting both genders is misguided male skill evaluation. In denigrating intuition, men do not realize that they are devaluing something of great importance in their own thinking; they think, wrongly, that it is only the women they are 'doing down'. However, their devaluing of this attribute rebounds badly on them. It is a similar picture in the case of know-how and skills.

Incidentally, feminism is often thought of as a set of beliefs that involves nothing but taking from men to give to women. This is often not the case. For example, we have just seen that feminists, in drawing attention to the need for AI to incorporate intuition and 'knowing how', benefit not only themselves but also those who set out to devalue them. Women can call for a generous concern for others unlike those who practise the partisan aggression of men.

Radical level testing of computing is likely to call for radically new developments and we mentioned earlier that, unsurprisingly, it is not possible in principle to predict such fundamentally new developments. It is consequently impossible at this point to predict the outcome of the find-a-new-science solution. As Elizabeth Fee points out:

> For us to imagine a feminist science in a feminist society is rather like asking a medieval peasant to imagine the theory of genetics or the production of a space capsule (Fee 1983, p22).

What does seem certain is that many opportunities to find-a-new-science and to make computing a gender-free subject will arise. What is sorely needed is the will to seize them.

## 12.5   The Beginning . . .

I have been arguing that we should not rest content at the add-more-women level but should move on to the liberal level. I have been trying, groping, to identify a level beyond the liberal to which we should also aspire, whatever it may be. In saying this I am not suggesting that one level supersedes or replaces another – they are complementary and the relationship between them is quite complex. Success at the add-more-women level, for instance, should greatly enhance the possibility of success at the liberal level. And that, in turn, would feed back to the add-more-women level. Moreover, success at the liberal and radical levels could well be contemporaneous; neither these two levels, nor any levels, have to occur in sequence.

# Appendix A

# Statistics

This appendix provides the statistical foundation for Chapter 6. I have removed the raw statistics and much of the detailed description of them from that chapter to smooth the reading of it.

This appendix consists of four sections. The first two give data on a single typical national cohort of students taking the General Certificate of Secondary Education or GCSE in Computer Studies in 1990 and Advanced or 'A' level in 1992 and entering university in that same year. The third section gives details of a survey I conducted for this book. It gives employment statistics from some universities: the numbers of men and women in junior and senior posts. In order to be promoted in the academic world, one has to publish, so the final section is about publications and the publication rates for women and for men.

## A.1   Secondary Education

First I should remind readers that the statistics given for secondary education examinations are for England, Wales and Northern Ireland only – Scotland has a different system.

Figure A.1 shows GCSE attempts and passes at higher grades in computer studies for 15- and 16-year-old girls and boys. In 1990 39.5% of attempts at GCSE computer studies were made by girls compared to 60.5% by boys. Of those achieving grades A–C 41.5% were girls and 58.5% were boys.

Figure A.2 shows 'A' level attempts and passes in computer studies for school leavers taken two years later by the same cohort. Only 17.3% of those attempting and 15.8% of those passing this examination are female (SOE 1991 & 1993). So already between the ages of 16 and 18 the enthusiasm of girls for this subject had begun to wane.

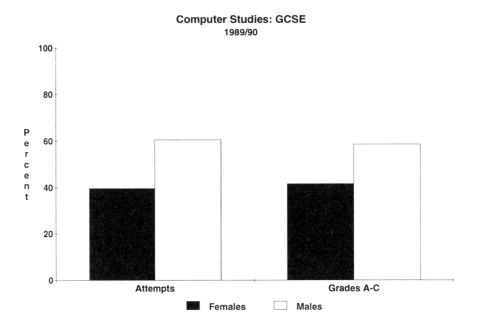

**Figure A.1:** *Computer Studies: GCSE Level*

## A.2   Higher Education

The trend for females to opt out of computer studies continues as we move on to higher education. Figure A.3 shows the number of women and men students – full-time and 'home' (roughly speaking UK domiciled) – taking computer studies at undergraduate level in the whole of the UK over the period starting with the academic year 1988/89 through to 1992/93. The number of women studying the subject nearly doubled over this five year period, rising from 484 to 914. The number of men, on the other hand, increased from 4651 to 6570.

Figure A.4 shows the *percentage* figures of female and male undergraduates for all disciplines and the percentage figures for computer studies in the same years (USR 1988–93). (These are for students attending the 'old' universities, that is those in existence before the former polytechnics were 'upgraded' to university status in 1992. The reason in this instance is that the only figures obtainable for polytechnic students included those taking either maths or computer studies. To include maths students confuses the data. To get meaningful statistics it is necessary to operate within a narrow definition of computer studies which excludes, for example,

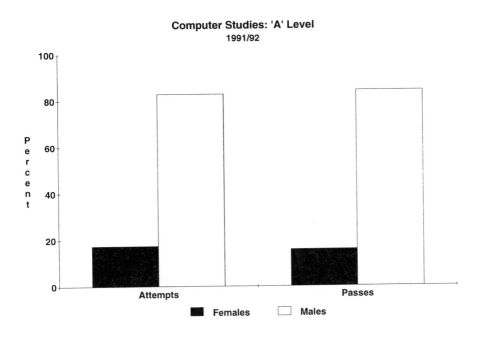

**Figure A.2:** *Computer Studies: 'A' Level*

students taking computing with another subject and those taking information systems.)

It will be seen from Figure A.4 that the percentage of women undergraduates in all disciplines is becoming equal to the percentage of men, rising over the five years in question from 44.2 to 48.4. This figure also shows that the percentage of female computer studies undergraduates is rising too, but from the abysmal figure of 9.4 to 12.2 – an increase which does little to put right so great an imbalance.

There is evidence that the figure of 12.2% for women has started to drop. Statistics for 24 'old' universities in the UK for 1993/94, again for home students studying computing alone and not in combination with another subject, show that the percentage of women had dropped to 10.9 (CPHC 1994).

## A.3    University Statistics 1991/92 – Academic Staff

Requests for gendered lists of staff and publication lists for the academic year 1991/92 were sent to computing departments in 57 'old' universities. Of the 41 replies, 38 provided gendered staff lists and, of these 38, 28 gave both gendered lists

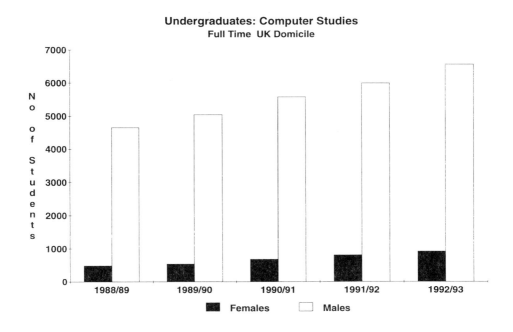

**Figure A.3:** *Numbers of University Undergraduates taking Computer Studies*

and publication lists. Table A.1 shows the numbers of men and women on each of the academic salary scales in these 28 'old' UK universities which provided gendered staff lists and publication lists. Table A.2 shows this same data but aggregated and with row percentages added. 'Senior' in this table means professors, readers and senior lecturers. 'Junior' means lecturers, senior research fellows and research fellows ('SRF & RF'). In neither of these tables are computing assistants, research assistants or tutors included, nor are part-time staff.

The 'new' universities in the UK have a different nomenclature for most of these positions. These can be broadly compared as follows: professors are equivalent in both types of institution, readers and senior lecturers are known as principal lecturers in the 'new' universities. A lecturer in an 'old' university who is earning a salary in the top part of the salary scale is equivalent to a senior lecturer in a 'new' university. The bottom part of the lecturers' scale in the 'old' universities corresponds to lecturer grade in both kinds of institution.

In the US, and other countries, terminology can be compared with that of the 'old' UK universities as follows: professors in the UK are the equivalent of full professors in the US, senior lecturers and readers are the equivalent of associate professors,

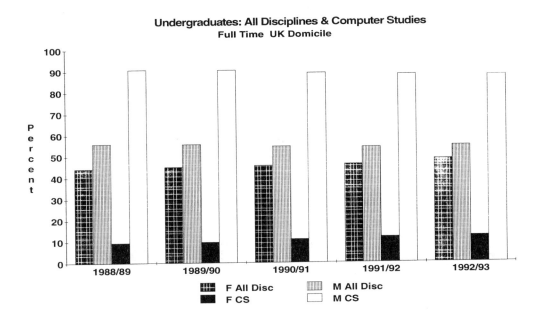

**Figure A.4:** *Percentage of Female/Male University Undergraduates in All Disciplines and Female/Male in Computer Studies*

lecturers are assistant professors. Again these comparisons are somewhat rough and ready.

Returning to the present survey of 1991/92, 13.4% of junior staff were women and this drops to 6% for senior staff. Thus only 10.7% of academic staff at all levels working in computer science in this sample were female. Of these few women, the vast majority (80%) were employed at the lower levels.

Of the university computing departments surveyed, 18% employed no women at all at the academic level, and of the 82% who employed at least one woman, only 46% of departments had more than one. The significance of these figures must be seen in light of the fact that a medium size department generally consists of about 20 academics. In 1991/92, only one computer science department had a female head.

Table A.3 gives the percentages of junior and senior staff for *all* universities from 1987/88 through 1992/93 which figured in the Universities Statistical Record (USR). Here, however, the category of 'Junior' includes what the USR calls 'Other grades' which is wider than the 'SRF & RF' category that appears in tables A.1 and A.2. A comparison of table A.2 with table A.3 shows that moving from the analysis of

| Grade | Women | Men | Total |
|---|---|---|---|
| Professor | 3 | 88 | 91 |
| Reader | 3 | 21 | 24 |
| Senior Lecturer | 7 | 94 | 101 |
| Lecturer | 43 | 315 | 358 |
| SRF & RF | 8 | 15 | 23 |

**Table A.1:** *Academic Computing Staff in 28 Universities 1991/92*

|  | Women | Men | Total |
|---|---|---|---|
| Senior | 13 | 203 | 216 |
| % | 6.0 | 94.0 | 100.0 |
| Junior | 51 | 330 | 381 |
| % | 13.4 | 86.6 | 100.0 |
| Total | 64 | 533 | 597 |
| % | 10.7 | 89.3 | 100.0 |

**Table A.2:** *Aggregation of Data in Table A.1*

staff by grade and gender in 28 universities to a similar analysis of the wider set of all the universities gives, for the academic year 1991/92, a worse figure (5.2%) for senior staff and a better figure (16.2%) for junior staff. The difference in junior staff could be due to the fact that more categories are included in the USR statistics. Introducing the 'new' universities as well could cause some change in the profile.

|  | Junior | | Senior | | Total | |
|---|---|---|---|---|---|---|
| Year | Women | Men | Women | Men | Women | Men |
| 1987/88 | 12.7 | 87.3 | 3.7 | 96.3 | 11.0 | 89.0 |
| 1988/89 | 12.3 | 87.7 | 4.0 | 96.0 | 10.7 | 89.3 |
| 1989/90 | 14.0 | 86.0 | 3.9 | 96.1 | 12.0 | 88.0 |
| 1990/91 | 15.3 | 84.7 | 4.4 | 95.6 | 13.2 | 86.8 |
| 1991/92 | 16.2 | 83.3 | 5.2 | 94.8 | 13.9 | 86.1 |
| 1992/93 | 14.5 | 85.5 | 5.7 | 94.3 | 12.7 | 87.3 |

**Table A.3:** *Percentage of Academic Computing Staff by Gender in all Universities (USR)*

Some argue that the ratio of women at junior level to those at senior level is so considerable, not because of biased promotion policies but because there has been a recent surge of appointments of women to junior posts and these women are not yet within range of promotion. The first column in table A.3 and figure A.5 show that there has not been any such surge – there is even a small drop in 1992/93.

**Computer Studies Staff**

**Junior and Senior Staff by Gender**

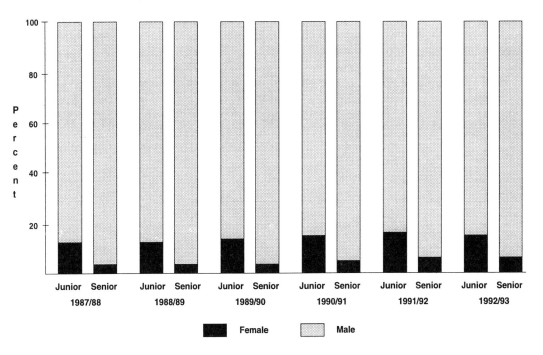

**Figure A.5:** *Computer Studies Staff*

## A.4 Publications

This section on publications is in two parts. The first part is based on publication lists and gendered staff lists from the 28 universities referred to at the beginning of section A.3. It details the numbers of different types of publications written by women and men as recorded in reports produced annually by computer science departments. The second part describes two further small surveys of the gender distribution of the authorship of books and articles. But, this time, the data comes from other sources and involves authors outside as well as inside the universities.

### A.4.1 Annual Reports from Computer Science Departments 1990/92

The lists of publications obtained from 28 universities varied in the periods they covered and in what they included. Some were for calendar years, some for academic years and in some cases they covered one year and in others, two. These statistics fall within the period 1990 to 1992.

The results obtained are shown in table A.4 where 'Articles, etc.' includes articles in academic journals, both refereed and unrefereed, contributions to conference proceedings, chapters in academic books and editorship of academic books e.g. conference proceedings and other collections of papers. It does not include technical reports. (Those included are the CVCP/UFC categories 02, 03, 04, 05, 07, 10, 11, 15.)

Where an item has multiple authors, each of the authors is credited with a published item. So a paper with three authors whose names appear in the staff list in the categories of academic staff used in tables A.1 and A.2 is included three times. The same rule applies to books. Although research in the past was perhaps not given so much importance in the 'new' universities as in the 'old', there is no reason to suppose that men and women in the 'new' universities publish in a different ratio to that in the 'old'.

Table A.4 shows that women published 7.7% of articles, conference papers and contributions to books and wrote 3.0% of books while the proportion of women computing academics at that time was 10.7%.

|               | Women | Men  | Total |
|---------------|------:|-----:|------:|
| Articles, etc. |   158 | 1882 |  2040 |
| %             |   7.7 | 92.3 | 100.0 |
| Books         |     1 |   33 |    34 |
| %             |   3.0 | 97.0 | 100.0 |

**Table A.4:** *Publications by Gender from 28 universities*

## A.4.2   Other Sources of Publication Statistics

**Books 1993**

There are of course other sources of statistics on the proportion of computing books written by women. The 1993 catalogues of two major publishers of academic computing texts list 903 books by named authors. The gender of the author could be inferred for 805 (the gender of the remainder could not be determined). Of these, 8% were by one or more female authors, 82.1% by one or more male authors, 9.9% were jointly written by women and men (McGraw-Hill 1993, Addison-Wesley 1993). Splitting the jointly-authored works equally between the genders, 12.9% of books on computing were written by women.

There are several strong caveats to these statistics. One is that the authors were from all over the world and the proportion of authorship of books by women in this worldwide scene may not be reflected in the UK. Moreover, some of them worked in industry and in government organisations so were not members of the academic profession.

**Journal Publications 1988-93**

Issues of five computing journals from the beginning of 1988 to mid-1993 (i.e. just over five years) were examined. The journals chosen (on databases, data engineering

| | Men only | Women only | Men and Women M 1st | W 1st | Total | Gender unknown |
|---|---|---|---|---|---|---|
| DKE | 81 | 5 | 10 | 8 | 104 | 20 |
| % | 77.9 | 4.8 | 9.6 | 7.6 | 100.0 | |
| IEEE/SE | 452 | 23 | 54 | 39 | 568 | 4 |
| % | 79.6 | 4.1 | 9.5 | 6.9 | 100.0 | |
| IEEE/DKE | 123 | 4 | 19 | 10 | 156 | 0 |
| % | 78.9 | 2.6 | 12.2 | 6.4 | 100.0 | |
| ACMTODS | 53 | 2 | 3 | 5 | 63 | 44 |
| % | 84.1 | 3.2 | 4.8 | 7.9 | 100.0 | |
| SPE | 208 | 1 | 16 | 13 | 238 | 126 |
| % | 87.4 | 0.4 | 6.7 | 5.5 | 100.0 | |
| Total | 917 | 35 | 102 | 75 | 1129 | 194 |
| % | 81.2 | 3.1 | 9.0 | 6.6 | 100.0 | |

**Table A.5:** *Gender Distribution of Authorship of Articles of Five Selected Journals*

and software engineering) were those specialising in topics where one would expect women, on the whole, to publish more than in other journals on, for example, neural networks and those oriented towards hardware topics.

The five journals were:

DKE — *Data and Knowledge Engineering*, Vols 3–9; Vol 10, Nos 1, 2

IEEE/SE — *IEEE Transactions on Software Engineering*, Vols 15–18; Vol 19, Nos 1, 2

IEEE/DKE — *IEEE Transactions on Data and Knowledge Engineering*, Vols 1–4; Vol 5, No 1 (This journal commenced publication in 1989)

ACMTODS — *ACM Transactions on Databases*, Vols 13–17; Vol 18, No 1

SPE — *Software Practice and Experience*, Vols 18–22; Vol 23, Nos 1–6

The gender of all authors in SPE and ACMTODS was inferred. In the IEEE and later editions of DKE, biographies and photographs identified the gender of most authors. In tables A.5 and A.6 'Men only' and 'Women only' mean 'one or more men' and 'one or more women'. 'First' author as in 'M 1st' and 'W 1st' means that a man's or woman's name literally appeared first in the list of authors.

Table A.6 is a summary form of table A.5 and shows that the proportion of articles written by one or more women authors, or written by both men and women where a woman was the first author, was 9.7%.

Again, as in the case of books, it does not follow that statistics from this source reflect the number of publications by the UK academic community; authors for these

|              | Men only + Man 1st author | Women only + Woman 1st author | Total |
|--------------|--------------------------:|------------------------------:|------:|
| DKE          | 91                        | 13                            | 104   |
| %            | 87.5                      | 12.5                          | 100.0 |
| IEEE/SE      | 506                       | 62                            | 568   |
| %            | 89.1                      | 10.9                          | 100.0 |
| IEEE/DKE     | 142                       | 14                            | 156   |
| %            | 91.0                      | 9.0                           | 100.0 |
| ACMTODS      | 56                        | 7                             | 63    |
| %            | 88.9                      | 11.1                          | 100.0 |
| SPE          | 224                       | 14                            | 238   |
| %            | 94.1                      | 5.9                           | 100.0 |
| Total        | 1019                      | 110                           | 1129  |
| %            | 90.3                      | 9.7                           | 100.0 |

**Table A.6:** *Distribution by Gender of Only and First Authors*

journals come from all over the world, not just the UK. Moreover, not all of them work in the academic hierarchy. Nonetheless, these statistics are very roughly in line with those gleaned from my sample of the 'old' universities' annual reports, though whether these statistics would square with those from the former polytechnics is unknown.

# Bibliography

**Adam, Alison** (1994) 'Who Knows How? Who Knows What? Feminist Epistemology and Artificial Intelligence', *in* Adam et al. (1994).

**Adam, Alison, Emms, Judy, Green, Eileen and Owen, Jenny** (eds.) (1994) *Proceedings of the Conference on Women, Work and Computerization 1994*, North-Holland.

**Addison-Wesley** (1993) *The Complete Computing Catalogue*, Wokingham, Berkshire: Addison-Wesley.

**Armstrong, Jane M.** (1981) 'Achievement and Participation of Women in Mathematics: Results of Two National Surveys', *Journal for Research in Mathematics Education*, **12**(5), pp. 356–72.

**Bacon, Francis** (1870) 'De Dignitate et Augmentis', *in* James Spedding (ed.), *Works*, vol. 4, London: Longman Green.

**Baker Miller, Jean** (1991) 'The Development of Women's Sense of Self', *in* J. V. Jordan, A. G. Kaplan, J. B. Miller, I. P. Stiver and J. L. Surrey (eds.), *Women's Growth in Connection: Writings From the Stone Centre*, New York: The Guilford Press, Chapter 1, pp. 11–26.

**Battel, Róisín Ní Mháille** (1994) 'Women and Technology: A Place for Hardware', *in* A. Adam and J. Owen (eds.), *Proceedings of the 5th IFIP International Conference on Women, Work and Computerization 'Breaking Old Boundaries Building New Forms'*, Conference Papers, pp. 397–404.

**BCS** (1988) *Guide to Applications for C.Eng and I.Eng*, The British Computer Society.

**Bennett, Sheila Kishler** (1982) 'Student Perceptions of and Expectations for Male and Female Instructors: Evidence Relating to the Question of Gender Bias in Teaching Evaluation', *Journal of Educational Psychology*, **74**(2), pp. 170–9.

**Berg, Anne-Jorunn** (1994) 'A Gendered Socio-technical Construction: The Smart House', *in* C. Cockburn and R. F. Dilić (eds.), *Bringing Technology Home: Gender and Technology in a Changing Europe*, Milton Keynes: Open University Press, pp. 165–80.

**Berge, Z. L.** (1987) *Effect of Group Size on Learning Science Process Skills Using Microcomputers*, Dissertation Proposal, Michigan State University.

**Bleier, Ruth** (1988) '*Science* and the Construction of Meanings in the Neurosciences', *in* S. V. Rosser (ed.), *Feminism within Science and Health Care Professions: Overcoming Resistance*, Oxford: Pergamon Press.

**BT** (1992) *BT Martlesham Research Reports on Teleworking*, British Telecom.

**Butler, Linda** (1993) 'Unpaid Work: What People Do at Home and in the Community', *The TEC Director*, November, **17**, pp. 26–7.

**CACM** (1990) 'Women and Computing', *Communications of the Association for Computing Machinery*, **33**(11).

**CACM** (1995) 'Special Edition on Women in Computing', *Communications of the Association for Computing Machinery*, **38***(1)*.

**Cameron, Deborah** (1985) *Feminism and Linguistic Theory*, London: Macmillan.

**Chalmers, A.F.** (1978) *What is This Thing Called Science?* Milton Keynes: Open University Press.

**Clarke, Valerie A. and Chambers, Susan M.** (1989) 'Gender-based Factors in Computing Enrollments and Achievement: Evidence from a Study of Tertiary Students', *Journal of Educational Computing Research*, **5**(4), pp. 409–29.

**Cockburn, Cynthia** (1985) *Machinery of Dominance: Women, Men and Technical Know-How*, London: Pluto Press.

**Cockburn, Cynthia and Ormrod, Susan** (1993) *Gender and Technology in the Making*, Newbury Park, CA and London: Sage.

**Cocks, Joan** (1984) 'Wordless Emotions: Some Critical Reflections on Radical Feminism', *Politics and Society*, **13**(1), pp. 27–57.

**Collis, Betty** (1987) 'Sex Differences in the Association Between Secondary School Students' Attitudes Toward Mathematics and Toward Computers', *Journal for Research in Mathematics Education*, **18**(5), pp. 394–402.

**CPHC** (1994) *Computer Science Directory*, Conference of Professors and Heads of Computing.

**Critical Eye** (1994) Service With a Smile, *Channel 4*, 15 September.

**Culley, Lorraine** (1986) *Gender Differences and Computing in Secondary Schools*, Technical report, Department of Education, Loughborough University, Leicestershire, UK.

**Dreyfus, Hubert L. and Dreyfus, Stuart E.** (1986) *Mind over Machine*, New York: The Free Press.

**Edwards, Paul N.** (1990) 'The Army and the Microworld: Computers and the Politics of Gender Identity', *Signs: Journal of Women in Culture and Society*, **16**(1), pp. 102–27.

**EIU** (1993) *Toys in the UK*, Economist Intelligence Unit.

**Elkan, Charles and Greiner, Russell** (1993) Book Review 'Building Large Knowledge-Based Systems: Representation and Inference in the Cyc Project', *Artificial Intelligence*, **61**, pp. 41–52.

**EOC** (1985) *Infotech and Gender: An Overview*, Equal Opportunities Commission.

**Eriksson, I.V., Kitchenham, B.A. and Tijdens, K.G.** (eds.) (1991) *Proceedings of the Conference on Women, Work and Computerization 1991*, North-Holland.

**Etzkowitz, Henry, Kemelgor, Carol, Neuschatz, Michael, Uzzi, Brian and Alonzo, Joseph** (1994) 'The Paradox of Critical Mass for Women in Science', *Science*, **266**, pp. 51–4.

**Fee, Elizabeth** (1983) 'Women's Nature and Scientific Objectivity', *in* M.Lowe and R. Hubbard (eds.), *Women's Nature: Rationalization of Inequality*, New York: Pergamon Press.

**Fischer, Claude S.** (1988) ' "Touch Someone": The Telephone Industry Discovers Sociability', *Technology and Culture*, **29**(1), pp. 32–61.

**Francis, Leslie J.** (1994) 'The Relationship Between Computer Related Attitudes and Gender Stereotyping of Computer Use', *Computers and Education*, **22**(4), pp. 283–9.

**GABe, Frances** (1983) 'The GABe Self-Cleaning House', *in* J. Zimmerman (ed.), *Technological Woman*, Praeger, pp. 75–82.

**Gilligan, Carol** (1993) *In a Different Voice: Psychological Theory and Women's Development*, 2nd edn, Harvard University Press.

**Gray, Peter M.D.** (1984) *Logic, Algebra and Databases*, Chichester: Ellis-Horwood.

**Green, Eileen, Owen, Jenny and Pain, Den** (1991) 'Developing Computerised Office Systems: A Gender Perspective in UK Approaches', *in* Eriksson et al. (1991), pp. 217–32.

**Greenbaum, Joan** (1990) 'The Head and the Heart: Using gender analysis to study the social construction of computer systems', *Computers and Society*, **20**(2), pp. 9–17.

**Gries, David and Marsh, Dorothy** (1992) 'The 1989–90 Taulbee Survey', *Communications of the Association for Computing Machinery*, **35**(1), pp. 133–42.

**Gunter, Karen** (1994) 'Women and the Information Revolution: Washed Ashore by the Third Wave', *in* Adam et al. (1994), pp. 439–52.

**Hacker, Sally** (1981) 'The Culture of Engineering: Woman, Workplace, and Machine', *Women's Studies International Quarterly*, **4**(3), pp. 341–53.

**Haddon, Leslie and Silverstone, Roger** (1994) *Teleworking in the 1990s: A View from the Home*, Technical report, Department of Media Studies, Sussex University, UK.

**Harding, Sandra** (1986) *The Science Question in Feminism*, New York: Cornell University Press.

**Harding, Sandra** (1991) *Whose Science? Whose Knowledge? Thinking from Women's Lives*, Milton Keynes: Open University Press.

**Harding, Stella** (1993) *'Coming of Age' in Software Engineering?: The Rhetoric of Professionalism in Formal Discourse*, Technical report, Social and Computer Sciences Research Group, Department of Sociology, University of Surrey, Guildford.

**Hearn, Jeff** (1989) *The Sexuality of Organisation*, London: Sage.

**Heinssen, Robert K., Glass, Carol R. and Knight, Luanne A.** (1987) 'Assessing Computer Anxiety: Development and Validation of the Computer Anxiety Rating Scale', *Computers in Human Behavior*, **3**(1), pp. 49–59.

**Hess, Robert B. and Miura, Irene T.** (1985) 'Gender Differences in Enrolment in Computer Camps and Classes', *Sex Roles*, **13**(3/4), pp. 193–203.

**Hodges, Andrew** (1985) *The Enigma of Intelligence*, Counterpoint, Unwin Paperbacks.

*Horizon* (1993) 'The Electronic Frontier', BBC2, 7 June.

**Hoyles, Celia** (1988) Review of the literature, *in* C. Hoyles (ed.), *Girls and Computers*, University of London: Institute of Education, pp. 5–12.

**Igbaria, Magid, Schiffman, Stephen J. and Wieckowski, Thomas J.** (1994) 'The Respective Roles of Perceived Usefulness and Perceived Fun in the Acceptance of Microcomputer Technology', *Behaviour and Information Technology*, **13**(6), pp. 349–61.

**Jay, Timothy B.** (1981) 'Computerphobia: What to Do about It', *Educational Technology*, **21**, pp. 47–8.

**Jordanova, L.J.** (1980) 'Natural Facts: A Historical Perspective on Science and Sexuality', *in* C. MacCormack and M. Strathern (eds.), *Nature, Culture and Gender*, Cambridge: Cambridge University Press.

**Jung, C. G. and Pauli, W.** (1955) *The Interpretation of Nature and the Psyche*, London: Routledge and Kegan Paul.

**Kanter, Rosabeth Moss** (1977) *Men and Women of the Corporation*, New York: Basic Books.

**Keller, Evelyn Fox** (1983) 'Women, Science and Popular Mythology', *in* J. Rothschild (ed.), *Machina ex Dea*, New York: Pergamon Press.

**Kierstead, Diane, D'Agostino, Patti and Dill, Heidi** (1988) 'Sex Role Stereotyping of College Professors: Bias in Students' Ratings of Instructors', *Journal of Educational Psychology*, **80**(3), pp. 342–4.

**Kiesler, Sara, Sproull, Lee and Eccles, Jacquelynne S.** (1985) 'Pool Halls, Chips, and War Games: Women in the Culture of Computing', *Psychology of Women Quarterly*, **9**(4), pp. 451–62.

**Kosko, Bart** (1994) *Fuzzy Thinking: The New Science of Fuzzy Logic*, London: HarperCollins.

**Kraft, Philip** (1979) 'The Industrialisation of Computer Programming', *in* A.Zimbalist (ed.), *Case Studies on the Labor Process*, Monthly Review Press.

**Kramer, Pamela E. and Lehman, Sheila** (1990) 'Mismeasuring Women: A Critique of Research on Computer Ability and Avoidance', *Signs: Journal of Women in Culture and Society*, **16**(1), pp. 158–72.

**Laver, Murray** (1980) *Computers and Social Change*, Cambridge Computer Science Texts 10, Cambridge: Cambridge University Press.

**Lavington, Simon** (1980) *Early British Computers*, Manchester University Press.

**Lavington, Simon** (1985) 'Qualified Binary Relationship Model', *in* A.F. Grundy (ed.), *Proceedings of Fourth British National Conference on Databases*, Cambridge: Cambridge University Press.

**Lenat, Douglas B and Guha, R.V.** (1989) *Building Large Knowledge-Based Systems: Representation and Inference in the Cyc Project*, Wokingham, Berkshire: Addison-Wesley.

**Lever, Janet** (1976) 'Sex Differences in the Games Children Play', *Social Problems*, **23**, pp. 478–87.

**LFS** (1991) *Labour Force Survey, 1991*, EOC Statistics Unit.

**Lifestyle Software Group** (n.d.) *Betty Crocker's Cookbook*, St Augustine, FL: Lifestyle Software Group.

**Linn, Marcia C.** (1985) 'Gender Equity in Computer Learning Environments', *Computers and the Social Sciences*, **1**(1), pp. 19–27.

**Loomis, Mary** (1987) *Database Systems*, New York: Macmillan Publishing.

**Lovegrove, Gillian and Segal, Barbara D.** (eds.) (1991) *Women into Computing: Selected Papers 1988–1990*, Oxford: Springer-Verlag.

**Luria, Z.** (1981) *Presentation at the Dedication Conference*, Technical report, Wellesley College, Wellesley, MA.

**MacKenzie, Donald and Wajcman, Judy** (1985) Introductory essay, *in* D. MacKenzie and J. Wajcman (eds.), *The Social Shaping of Technology*, Milton Keynes: Open University Press.

**Mandinach, Ellen B. and Linn, Marcia C.** (1987) 'Cognitive Consequences of Programming: Achievements of Experienced and Talented Programmers', *Journal of Educational Computing Research*, **3**(1), pp. 53–72.

**Martin, Elaine** (1984) 'Power an Authority in the Classroom: Sexist Stereotypes in Teaching Evaluations', *Signs: Journal of Women in Culture and Society*, **9**(3), pp. 482–92.

**Maurer, Matthew M.** (1994) 'Computer Anxiety Correlates and What They Tell Us: A Literature Review', *Computers in Human Behavior*, **10**(3), pp. 369–76.

**McGraw-Hill** (1993) *Computing Textbooks*, Maidenhead, Berkshire: McGraw-Hill.

**Merchant, Carolyn** (1980) *The Death of Nature: Women, Ecology and the Scientific Revolution*, New York: Harper and Row.

**Miles, Ian** (1988) *Home Informatics*, London: Pinter Publishers.

**Mill, Harriet Taylor** (1970*a*) 'The Enfranchisement of Women', *in* A. Rossi (ed.), *Essays on Sex Equality*, Chicago: University of Chicago Press.

**Mill, John Stuart** (1910) 'Letter to Alexander Bain, 14th July 1869', *in* H. S. Elliot (ed.), *The Letters of John Stuart Mill, vol 2*, London: Longmans, Green and Co.

**Mill, John Stuart** (1936) *A System of Logic Ratiocinative and Inductive*, London: Longmans, Green and Co.

**Mill, John Stuart** (1970*b*) 'The Subjection of Women', *in* A. Rossi (ed.), *Essays on Sex Equality*, Chicago: University of Chicago Press.

**Mill, John Stuart** (1984) The Subjection of Women, *in* J. M. Robson (ed.), *Collected Works of John Stuart Mill, Vol XXI, Essays on Equality, Law, and Education*, Toronto: University of Toronto Press.

**Moore, B.** (1986) *Equity in Education: Gender Issues in the Use of Computers in Education. A Review and Bibliography*, vol. 26, Ontario, Canada: Review and Evaluation Bulletins, Ministry of Education.

**Mumford, Enid** (1983) *Designing Secretaries*, Manchester Business School.

**Mumford, Enid and Henshall, Don** (1979) *A Participative Approach to Computer Systems Design*, Associated Business Press.

**Nelson, Lori J., Wiese, Gina M. and Cooper, Joel** (1991) 'Getting Started with Computers: Experience, Anxiety and Relational Style', *Computers in Human Behavior*, **7**(3), pp. 185–202.

**Newton, Peggy** (1991) 'Computing: An Ideal Occupation for Women?', *in* J. Firth-Cozens and M. West (eds.), *Women at Work: Psychological and Organisational Perspectives*, Milton Keynes: Open University Press, pp. 143–53.

**New Woman** (1993*a*) 'Tactics that Work', *New Woman*, March.

**New Woman** (1993*b*) 'The Voice of Reason', *New Woman*, February.

**Oxborrow, Elizabeth** (1989) *Databases and Database Systems: Concepts and Issues*, Bromley: Chartwell-Bratt.

**PC Format** (1993) 'Jobs for the Lads', *PC Format*, September, **24**, p. 102.

**PC Format** (1995) 'The Final Insult', *PC Format*, April, **43**, p. 170.

**Peltu, Malcolm** (1994) 'Back to the Future', *Computing*, 5 May, p. 45.

**Pratt, John** (1985) 'The Attitudes of Teachers', *in* J. Whyte, R. Deem, L. Kant and M. Cruickshank (eds.), *Girl Friendly Schooling*, London: Methuen, pp. 24–35.

**Rich, Adrienne** (1987) *Blood, Bread and Poetry: Selected Prose 1979-1985*, London: Virago Press.

**Rothschild, Joan** (1983) 'Technology, Housework, and Women's Liberation: A Theoretical Analysis', *in* J. Rothschild (ed.), *Machina ex Dea: Feminist Perspectives on Technology*, New York: Pergamon Press.

**Sanders, Donald H.** (1973) *Computers in Society: An Introduction to Information Processing*, New York: McGraw-Hill.

**Sanders, J.** (1990) 'Computer Equity for Girls: What Keeps It From Happening?', *in Proceedings of the IFIP, TC3 Fifth World Conference on Computers in Education*, pp. 181–5.

**Schwartz Cowan, Ruth** (1983) *More Work for Mother: The Ironies of Household Technology from the Open Hearth to the Microwave*, New York: Basic Books.

**Smith, Sydney** (1840) Female Education, *in Works, Vol 1*, London: Longman, *et al.*

**SOE** (1991 & 1993) *Statistics of Education 1989/90 and 1991/92. Schools Examinations GCSE and GCE*, Department for Education.

**Sommerville, Ian, Rodden, Tom, Sawyer, Pete, Bentley, Richard and Twidale, Michael** (1992) *Integrating Ethnography into the Requirements Engineering Process*, Technical Report CSCW/17/92, Centre for Research in CSCW, Computing Department, Lancaster University, UK.

**Spavold, Janet** (1990) 'Observations of Attitudes to IT in Database Use in Schools', *in* G. Lovegrove and B. Segal (eds.), *Women into Computing: Selected Papers 1988–1990*, Oxford: Springer-Verlag, pp. 109–18.

**Spear, Margaret Goddard** (1985) 'Teachers' Attitudes Towards Girls and Technology', *in* J. Whyte, R. Deem, L. Kant and M. Cruickshank (eds.), *Girl Friendly Schooling*, London: Methuen, pp. 36–44.

**Spender, Dale** (1990)  *Man Made Language,* 3rd edn, London: Pandora Press.

**Spender, Dale** (1995)  *Nattering on the Net,* North Melbourne, Victoria: Spinifex.

**Stiver, Irene P.** (1991)  'The Meaning of Care: Reframing Treatment Models', *in* J. V. Jordan, A. G. Kaplan, J. B. Miller, I. P. Stiver and J. L. Surrey (eds.), *Women's Growth in Connection: Writings From the Stone Centre,* New York: The Guilford Press, Chapter 15, pp. 250–67.

**Storr, Anthony** (1960)  *The Integrity of the Personality,* Harmondsworth, Middx: Penguin Books.

**Straker, A.** (1985)  *MEP Primary Project Progress Report No.4.*

**Strok, Dale** (1992)  'Women in AI', *IEEE Expert,*  pp. 7–22.

**Tong, Rosemarie** (1989)  *Feminist Thought: A Comprehensive Introduction,* London: Routledge.

**Toole, Betty A.** (1992)  *Ada, the Enchantress of Numbers,* Mill Valley, CA: Strawberry Press.

**Turkle, Sherry** (1984*a*)  *The Second Self: Computers and the Human Spirit,* London: Granada.

**Turkle, Sherry** (1984*b*)  'Women and Computer Programming: A Different Approach', *Technology Review,*  pp. 48–50.

**Turkle, Sherry and Papert, Seymour** (1990)  'Epistemological Pluralism: Styles and Voices within the Computer Culture', *Signs: Journal of Women in Culture and Society,*  **16**(1), pp. 128–57.

**USR** (1988–93)  *University Statistics 1988-89, 1989-90, 1990-91, 1991-92, 1992-3; vol 1, Students and Staff.*

**Vanek, Joann** (1974)  'Time Spent on Housework', *Scientific American,*  **231**, pp. 116–20.

**Vehviläinen, Marja** (1991)  'Gender in Information Systems Development – a Women Office Workers' Standpoint', *in* Eriksson et al. (1991), pp. 247–62.

**Wajcman, Judy** (1991)  *Feminism Confronts Technology,* Cambridge: Polity Press.

**Weil, Michelle M., Rosen, Larry D. and Wugalter, Stuart E.** (1990)  'The Etiology of Computerphobia', *Computers in Human Behavior,*  **6**(4), pp. 361–79.

**Weinberg, Sanford B. and Fuerst, Mark Lawrence** (1984)  *Computerphobia: How to Slay the Dragon,* Wayne, PA: Banbury Books.

**Willcocks, Leslie and Marsh, David** (1987)  *Computerising Work: People, Systems Design and Workplace Relations,* London: Paradigm.

**WIT** (1992)  *The Nightmare Scenario. Spring 1992 Trends Report,* Farnborough, Hants: Women into Information Technology Foundation Ltd.

**Wittgenstein, Ludwig** (1922)  *Tractatus Logico-Philosophicus,* London: Routledge and Kegan Paul.

**Yourdon, Edward** (1993)  *The Decline and Fall of the American Programmer,* Englewood Cliffs, NJ: Yourdon Press, Prentice Hall.

**Zimmerman, Jan and Horwitz, Jaime** (1983)  'Living Better Vicariously?', *in* J. Zimmerman (ed.), *Technological Woman,* Praeger, pp. 113–21.

**Zuboff, Shoshana** (1988)  *The Age of the Smart Machine: The Future of Work and Power,* London: Heinemann Professional Publishing.

# Index